Environmental Economics: A Very Short Introduction

VERY SHORT INTRODUCTIONS are for anyone wanting a stimulating and accessible way in to a new subject. They are written by experts, and have been published in more than 25 languages worldwide.

The series began in 1995, and now represents a wide variety of topics in history, philosophy, religion, science, and the humanities. The VSI Library now contains 300 volumes—a Very Short Introduction to everything from ancient Egypt and Indian philosophy to conceptual art and cosmology—and will continue to grow in a variety of disciplines.

Very Short Introductions available now:

For more information visit our website
www.oup.com/vsi/

Stephen Smith

# ENVIRONMENTAL ECONOMICS

## A Very Short Introduction

OXFORD
UNIVERSITY PRESS

# OXFORD

## UNIVERSITY PRESS

Great Clarendon Street, Oxford OX2 6DP

Oxford University Press is a department of the University of Oxford.
It furthers the University's objective of excellence in research, scholarship,
and education by publishing worldwide in

Oxford New York

Auckland Cape Town Dar es Salaam Hong Kong Karachi
Kuala Lumpur Madrid Melbourne Mexico City Nairobi
New Delhi Shanghai Taipei Toronto

With offices in

Argentina Austria Brazil Chile Czech Republic France Greece
Guatemala Hungary Italy Japan Poland Portugal Singapore
South Korea Switzerland Thailand Turkey Ukraine Vietnam

Oxford is a registered trade mark of Oxford University Press
in the UK and in certain other countries

Published in the United States
by Oxford University Press Inc., New York

© Stephen Smith 2011

The moral rights of the author have been asserted
Database right Oxford University Press (maker)

First published 2011

British Library Cataloguing in Publication Data

Data available

Library of Congress Cataloging in Publication Data

Data available

Typeset by SPI Publisher Services, Pondicherry, India
Printed in Great Britain
on acid-free paper by
Ashford Colour Press Ltd, Gosport, Hampshire

ISBN 978–0–19–958358–4

1 3 5 7 9 10 8 6 4 2

# Contents

# Acknowledgements

This book aims to make the key ideas of environmental economics accessible to a wider public – to readers interested in the world in which we live, the relationship between economic activity and the environment, and the potential for environmental policy to improve the quality of life we and future generations can enjoy. It draws on the published work of many economists, and on discussions and policy debates in which I have participated over many years.

The late Professor David Pearce first inspired me to think about issues of environmental economics. I admired David's commitment to improving economic thinking about environmental policy, and I hope a little of his gift for clarity and communication has rubbed off on me, and might perhaps have found its way into this book.

Over the past two decades, I have discussed the issues in this book with successive generations of students at UCL, and have learned much from their experience, perceptive criticism, and environmental commitment.

I am grateful to my editors at OUP, Andrea Keegan and Emma Marchant, for their advice and encouragement, and to OUP's anonymous readers and Tony Allan for their careful reading and comments on the manuscript.

# Abbreviations

| | |
|---|---|
| $CO_2$ | **Carbon dioxide**, the principal greenhouse gas |
| CV | **Contingent valuation**, an approach for discovering the value that individuals place on things that do not have a market price (such as reductions in environmental harm), by directly asking people what they would be willing to pay in a hypothetical situation |
| EPA | The United States **Environmental Protection Agency** |
| EU ETS | The **European Union Emissions Trading System**, which limits industrial emissions of carbon dioxide using tradeable emissions quotas |
| FGD | **Flue gas desulphurization**, a technology for cleaning sulphur dioxide from power station emissions |
| MAC | **Marginal abatement cost**, the additional cost of reducing emissions by one more unit |
| MED | **Marginal environmental damage**, the additional environmental harm, measured in money terms, caused by one more unit of polluting emissions |
| OECD | **Organisation for Economic Co-operation and Development**, a forum for policy discussion among industrialized countries |
| $SO_2$ | **Sulphur dioxide**, the principal source of acid rain |
| WTP | **Willingness to pay**, the main form of questioning in contingent valuation studies, in which respondents are asked what they would be willing to pay for some non-traded good, such as some aspect of environmental quality, in a hypothetical market |

# List of illustrations

Environmental Economics

# Introduction

In very broad terms, environmental economics looks at how economic activity and policy affect the environment in which we live. Some production generates pollution – for example, power station emissions can cause acid rain and also contribute to global warming. Household consumption decisions too affect the environment – for example, more consumption can mean more waste sent to polluting incinerators or garbage dumps.

However, pollution is not an inevitable consequence of economic activity. Environmental policies can require polluting firms to clean up their emissions, and can encourage people to change their behaviour. Generally, though, these measures will involve some costs – of installing pollution control equipment, for example. So there's a tradeoff: a cleaner environment, but economic costs. The central questions in environmental economics concern this tradeoff:

- If environmental protection is costly, how much should we spend on pollution control? Is it worth reducing pollution to zero, or should we accept some level of pollution because of the economic benefits associated with it?
- In making these decisions, how can we assess the benefits that people get from a less-polluted environment?
- What form should government policies to cut pollution take? Should we adopt market-based environmental policies, using

pollution taxes or emissions trading to incentivize 'green' production and consumption?

Environmental economics provides a framework for thinking about these issues, which lie at the heart of such key areas of policy controversy and public debate as climate change, nuclear power, recycling, and traffic congestion.

# Chapter 1
# The economy and the environment

Londoners woke on the morning of Friday, 5 December 1952, to find the city blanketed by dense, yellowish, acidic fog – a 'smog' – that reduced visibility to barely a few yards and caught in the back of people's throats. The weather had been cold for some weeks, and the emissions of sulphurous soot from domestic coal fires, industry, and London's new diesel buses were trapped close to ground level by a layer of colder air – a temperature inversion that persisted for five days, until the winds changed direction. Much of the life of the city ground to a halt. Buses needed passengers with torches to walk in front of them to guide them home. Motorists followed the tail lights of the car in front, hoping that it was going in the right direction; some reportedly ended up in a stranger's front drive. Sporting events were cancelled as spectators would be unable to see the action on the pitch; the greyhound racing at White City was abandoned when the dogs could no longer see the mechanical hare they were supposed to chase. On the Saturday, a performance of *La Traviata* at Sadler's Wells was called off after the first act because the smog had seeped into the theatre and left the singers and audience coughing and choking.

London had long been known for its thick fogs – 'pea soupers' as the locals called them – but this was on a completely different scale, and had devastating consequences. Estimates at the time suggested that 4,000 people died as a result of the smog, though more recent estimates put the figure three times higher. Public outrage at the episode led directly to new legislation. The Clean Air Act of 1956 introduced smokeless zones in various parts of London, requiring householders to convert open coal fires to closed stoves burning smokeless fuels, or gas and electrical heaters, a measure that marked the start of the UK's modern pollution-control legislation.

Public anger forced a rapid policy response in the United States, too, a few years later, after the publication in 1962 of *Silent Spring*, by the biologist and naturalist Rachel Carson. In a meticulously researched and persuasively written account, Carson highlighted the drastic ecological effects of the practice of widespread and indiscriminate aerial spraying of DDT to kill mosquitoes. She argued that the poison was entering the wildlife food chain, and had led to a drastic fall in the population of birds and mammals over a wide area. Moreover, the effects threatened human health too, as residues entered the human food chain. The impact of the book was not simply a result of its observations on the harm to wildlife. Carson warned of the potential hazards that unregulated scientific innovations could pose for the environment, highlighting the misleading claims made by industry about the safety of their profitable new products and the uncritical acceptance of these by the public authorities. The outraged public response to the book led President Kennedy to initiate a Science Advisory Committee investigation of the book's claims. When this endorsed the book's message, radical policy action followed. The use of DDT was restricted and eventually banned, the powerful US Environmental Protection Agency was established in 1970, and a raft of tough new environmental legislation was introduced over the subsequent decade.

Both episodes – the 1952 London smog and the furore surrounding *Silent Spring* – signalled the emergence of widespread public concern about the environment as a major driver of policy action

1. London smog caused by severe atmospheric pollution: the Strand at midday, 17 November 1953

and legislation. The legislative actions that followed both events were by no means the first environmental legislation in either country. In the UK, industrial pollution had been regulated and controlled since the establishment of the Alkali Inspectorate in 1863. In the US, pollution regulation had largely been regarded as a matter for individual states rather than the federal government, but this had already begun to change, and the National Air Pollution Control Administration had been set up in 1955 in response to smog in Los Angeles and other problems. Nevertheless the two episodes were, perhaps, amongst the first signals of public recognition that issues of environmental quality are not simply technical issues of factory safety, but lie at the heart of our consumption and lifestyle, requiring changes in behaviour – and sometimes uncomfortable choices – across a wide field of public and private action.

Environmental economics provides a way of analysing these tradeoffs and choices. To policy-makers at the time, no doubt, the intensity of the public pressure for action made the policy decisions rather straightforward. With the benefit of hindsight, too, the actions taken seem a well-justified response to the problem. But both issues provide a useful illustration of the way in which environmental economics can help us to think about environmental policy choices, and shed light on some aspects of the underlying issues which are rather less straightforward.

The initial measures to control the London smog focused on restricting the use of coal for domestic heating. They required tough regulation of heating choices at the level of individual households, but supplemented this with substantial financial assistance to help households convert quickly from open coal fires to cleaner forms of heating. In the longer run, however, maintaining a clean atmosphere in London and other major cities has required a much broader portfolio of measures including emission regulations for motor vehicles, power stations, and industrial facilities. The costs of this programme of pollution abatement measures have been substantial, but set against the deaths, human distress, and massive disruption caused by smog in the 1950s the abatement costs seem well justified. London's atmosphere is now substantially cleaner than in 1952; levels of particulate pollution are now less than one-hundredth of the level in the early 1950s. Nevertheless, despite all the abatement expenditure, it has not been possible to entirely eliminate periods of poor air quality. In December 1991, another temperature inversion led to a freezing smog, containing a peak in concentration of pollutants from road transport well above safe levels, and, again, the death rate rose, albeit not as drastically as in 1952.

What would have to be done in order to eliminate completely the risk of any repetition of such pollution episodes? Clearly, further restrictions on emissions, and more wide-ranging restrictions on road transport and other private behaviour would be needed. How far should we go, in order to reduce the risk of any further period of high pollution? Would the costs involved be justified in terms of the benefits from eliminating the remaining risk? Questions of this sort lie at the heart of environmental economics, which provides a toolkit for structured thinking about this tradeoff, and for drawing a balance between the costs and benefits of further policy action.

Similarly, the policy response to *Silent Spring* prompts a question of how far to go in curbing the risks of environmental harm from the use of agricultural chemicals. The costs of reducing the damage caused by DDT are the costs of alternative forms of pest control, and, to the extent that the alternatives might be less effective, the loss of agricultural production and farm incomes. How far should we be willing to incur these abatement costs in order to achieve the benefits from eliminating the ecological harm to wildlife and the risks to human health? And at what point do we stop, and say that further costs are not justified in terms of reducing the remaining risks and harm?

The theme of this book is how to balance environmental and economic considerations in policy contexts such as these. In Chapter 2, we look at this choice. If, as it usually does, a cleaner environment comes at a cost, how should we decide whether

2. How should industrial development and environmental protection be balanced? Industrial pollution in the German Ruhrgebiet near Bottrop-Welheim in the 1960s, photographed by the industrial photographer Horst Lang (1931–2001)

the environmental gains justify the cost? This will rarely be an all-or-nothing choice, but a matter of the gains from a bit more pollution control, versus the additional costs incurred. Where should we draw the line?

In Chapter 3, we consider the policy instruments available to governments to regulate polluting emissions and environmental damage. Much environmental policy consists of legislation to prohibit environmentally damaging behaviour (such as a ban on using DDT), or to compel actions which will improve the environment (such as replacing open grates with cleaner domestic stoves and heaters). Economists have argued that direct and inflexible regulation of this sort can be unduly costly, and that the same environmental improvement could be achieved at lower

8

ost using more flexible, market-based forms of regulation.
hapter 3 looks at the case for this alternative approach.

hapter 4 considers further how we can weigh up environmental
ains against economic cost, by looking at ways to value
nvironmental benefits on a par with costs and benefits to which
arket prices are attached. There is a danger that what cannot be
alued gets ignored, or alternatively that it is treated as of
verriding importance, irrespective of the costs that might be
ncurred. Chapter 4 describes ways in which environmental
conomists have tried to capture the value that people place on
nvironmental quality, the quality of life, and other key factors
ntering into judgments about environmental policy.

hapter 5 then draws these lines of argument together, to look at
he most pressing environmental issue of our time, global
limate change. What is the economic case for action to limit global
limate change? How can we assess the benefits of action, not just
o ourselves, but also to future generations? What scale of action is
hen warranted, and how rapidly? Finally, what form should this
 action take? In particular, how far is there a role for pricing
nstruments such as carbon taxes and emissions trading in steering
ndividual behaviour towards lower-carbon choices?

## Why an unregulated market economy damages the environment

This is a book about *environmental* economics. But environmental
economics is embedded in the framework of ideas and methods
developed by economists more generally. To understand the
arguments of environmental economics, we need to begin by
briefly sketching in some of the general economics background to
the particular approaches taken in environmental economics.

Markets do many things well. They also do some things badly – in
some cases disastrously. Economists refer to these cases as

'market failure', and a lot of the economic justification for public policy action has to do with repairing the underlying causes of market failure, or mopping up the consequences. Nevertheless, to understand what economists mean by 'market failure' we first need to appreciate market success: what it is that markets do well when they function properly.

In principle, markets provide us with an extraordinarily efficient mechanism for allocating society's limited productive capacity – its stock of productive resources, including labour, capital, technology and natural resources – to their most highly valued uses.

Among the things that markets do well are that, by and large, they supply goods and services that consumers want. Firms that do not, go to the wall, while those that accurately identify consumer needs and desires and meet them will be more likely to make profits and thrive.

Competitive markets also allocate productive resources – labour and capital – to activities where they will be most productive. In doing this, prices coordinate economic activity in two crucial ways they communicate information about scarcity, and they incentivize behaviour that tends to make the most productive use of the available resources. Where something is in short supply, its price will tend to be bid up. The high price communicates this scarcity throughout the economic system, without the need for detailed information about the underlying origins or reasons for the scarce supply. The high price, too, is an incentive for a range of responses which will tend to reduce the scarcity: it will make additional supply profitable, it will choke off some demand, and it encourages innovation that may in due course create alternatives or reduce demand.

But markets do not always deliver such benign outcomes, and tracing the various forms of market failure is crucial to effective management and regulation of the economic system. Market

ilure does not, however, simply mean that the market economy
ads to outcomes that disappoint us. Rather, it means that there
e systematic impediments to the normal functioning of the
arket system, which have the effect that in some cases markets
ay not exist at all, and in other cases prices provide incentives
at fail to promote the common good.

ne way in which market failure can arise is when a market
articipant has monopoly power – as the only supplier, or one of a
ery limited number of suppliers of a particular good.
monopolist does not sell as many goods as can be profitably
roduced, but instead restricts supply, creating artificial scarcity
hich pushes prices up, in order to profit through higher prices
ather than maximum sales. Some consumer needs remain unmet,
ven though they could be met at a price which covers the costs
f supply.

Market failure can also arise where buyers and sellers in a
market have different knowledge about the characteristics of the
ood or service being sold. In some conditions, this can make it
mpossible for anyone to trade profitably, or for honest or
igh-quality producers to remain in the market. Market failure
lso arises in the supply of goods known as 'public goods', a
echnical term meaning goods which everyone benefits from as
oon as one person has bought them. Public street lighting would
e an example; we cannot selectively make the streets dark for
hose who have not paid for the lighting. In this situation, there is a
anger that no-one is willing to pay, and that all hope to free-ride
n their provision by others.

The economist's normal presumption that a market economy leads
o socially desirable outcomes is also overturned by the presence
f 'externalities', the category of market failure most directly
relevant to environmental policy. An externality is a situation
where the actions of some firm or individual have consequences
for someone else who has no say in the matter. Pollution is a

negative externality, where person A's actions cause harm to the interests of person B. City motorists cause noise and air pollution damaging the quality of life and possibly the health of people who live near urban roads, but an unregulated market economy does not require motorists' travel decisions to take this into account, and offers no route for the people harmed to choose the cleaner air that they want. A factory discharging toxic effluent into a lake may harm the livelihood of a fish-farmer, but the damage to the fish-farmer's profits do not enter into the calculation of the polluting factory's profits and its business decisions. Both are examples of negative pollution externalities, one affecting living standards, the other affecting a production activity.

Positive externalities can also arise; the classic case is the beekeeper whose hives of bees pollinate the fruit trees in a neighbouring orchard. In both cases, positive and negative, externalities are a source of 'market failure', in the sense that the natural operation of an unregulated market economy will not tend towards the efficient level of the externality. Without regulation, a market economy will have too few beekeepers, and it will have too much pollution.

To non-economist readers, it may seem like stating the obvious to observe that polluting firms harm people unless action is taken to stop them. But the key point about the notion of an externality as a market failure is that it pinpoints the source of the problem, and at the same time suggests possible remedies.

One thing should be clear: without some form of public intervention to regulate the level of pollution, we are unlikely to achieve the socially optimal level of pollution control. The reason for this is straightforward. The costs and benefits of pollution control accrue to different people. Installing pollution filters to reduce polluting emissions from industry would add to firms' costs (and reduce their profits), while the benefits would accrue to those harmed by pollution damage – local residents perhaps.

Unless there happens to be sufficient fortuitous benefit to polluting firms from reducing their pollution (in terms of good community relations, PR, or reputation), those bearing the costs of cutting pollution will not perceive corresponding benefits – and are therefore unlikely to be willing to pay for pollution control unless they are pushed into doing this by a government regulator.

# Chapter 2
# **The economic theory of efficient pollution control**

Let us start our exploration of environmental economics by tackling, head-on, the question that distinguishes the economic approach from many non-economic perspectives: 'What is the level of pollution that society should accept?' Or, to pose a related, but perhaps less provocative question: 'What level of resources should we devote to the reduction – the 'abatement' – of pollution?'

To some, these questions may seem easy to answer. Pollution is harmful and undesirable, and a civilized society should be willing to find the resources needed to eliminate it entirely. But let's push the question a little harder: If the price for reducing pollution is substantial, then how far should we go? Achieving a cleaner environment has a cost, in terms of the resources used to install and operate pollution-control equipment, the higher costs incurred in producing green goods instead of the cheapest alternative, and so forth. Some of these costs are likely to rise sharply, the more rigorously we try to control pollution. Is any level of pollution still unacceptable, even if eliminating pollution comes with an extremely high price tag?

Again, some may wish to avoid the question, by contesting the terms in which it is posed. It is sometimes contended that more stringent environmental policies would confer economic benefits –

by creating jobs, or enhancing innovation and economic growth, or by stimulating the export performance of firms making pollution control equipment. There is a germ of truth to each of these arguments, but none is sufficiently powerful to allow us to evade the fundamental question: in cases where pollution reductions come at a cost, how much cost are we willing to pay?

## The economist's answer

The economist's answer to these questions will typically involve weighing up the costs and benefits of each additional pound spent on pollution control: 'Does extra pollution control have benefits that are greater or less than what it will cost?' The costs include costs of pollution control equipment and the costs of changes in behaviour; the benefits include a range of effects on human health and quality of life.

Not all of these costs and benefits are easy to measure, and even where measurement techniques exist, they may be imprecise, and controversial. (Chapter 4 looks into the issue of measurement in more detail, and explores some of these controversies.) For the moment, however, we can obtain considerable insight into the economist's answer, without fully exploring the basis on which costs and benefits are measured. Two preliminary observations might, however, be made.

The first is that in assessing the case for pollution control in terms of its costs and benefits, we are not subtly restricting the range of considerations which carry weight in the analysis. In principle, all relevant costs and benefits need to be considered in this assessment, and not just those that involve money changing hands. Economics is about values, not simply about financial book-keeping. Health effects and aesthetic values are just as much part of the economic case for pollution control as, for example, the costs to firms of installing pollution filters, or the costs to municipalities of cleaning up a polluted environment.

Second, while the economic analysis aims to be comprehensive, it nevertheless uses money as the measure of value, a feature which is often – quite wrongly – held to imply that greater weight is given to some costs and benefits than others. Occasionally the economic approach is characterized as having concern only for business costs and profit, and caring nothing for the impact of pollution on the quality of life of ordinary citizens. Nothing could be further from the truth. Most of the energies of environmental economists have gone into devising ways to value – fully and comprehensively – those effects which lie outside normal market transactions. But the slander sticks – and we will need to return to explore these issues thoroughly in Chapter 4.

So, without necessarily having convinced the reader that our assessment of costs and benefits can, indeed, be comprehensive, or that all can legitimately be reduced to money values, let us explore the implications of this line of thinking, beginning with the simplest possible context. Consider a problem of local environmental pollution, generated perhaps by a factory chimney, discharging smoke and other pollutants into the local environment. Pollution control is possible by installing an abatement technology that, in effect, filters the chimney discharges, removing some proportion of the effluent. The technology of abatement allows for more or less effective filtering of the effluent, but cleaner discharges come at increasing cost. We could think, perhaps, of larger or more sophisticated filters being needed, or higher running costs if the effluent cleaning process is to remove a higher percentage of the polluting effluent. The upshot is that we face a range of possibilities for the percentage of pollution reduction, not just a binary 'yes or no?' decision. We can cut out more pollution, but only by incurring correspondingly higher abatement costs.

Set against the abatement costs of pollution control, we assess its benefits, in terms of the reduced pollution damage. At the risk of trivializing what can often be major issues of human health and wellbeing, let us suppose that the pollution damage in this case simply takes the form of corrosive dirt, which leads to a deterioration of motor vehicles, buildings, and other property. The greater the emissions level, the greater the level of dirt, and the greater the level of damage. Conversely, reducing emissions by increasing percentages leads to a correspondingly higher benefit in terms of the pollution damage avoided.

We can then ask how much pollution control would maximize the total net benefit to society, taking account both of the abatement costs incurred by the firm, and the benefits to local residents in terms of reduced pollution damage. Starting from the unrestricted initial situation, in which the factory can pump out as much effluent as it chooses, we can consider the implications of each successive step in restricting emissions, and at each successive notch on the pollution-control dial, ask whether the additional abatement confers sufficient additional benefits to justify incurring the extra cost.

To be precise about the question we are asking, a crucial piece of economic jargon is essential. We need to distinguish between the total costs of pollution abatement and the 'marginal' costs, in other words, the additional abatement cost from one extra unit of pollution abatement, starting from whatever level we have currently attained. Thus, for example, if we have already eliminated half of the emissions, the 'Marginal Abatement Cost' at that point is the extra cost of cutting one more unit of emissions (say one extra tonne of pollutant). Likewise, when we are considering the benefit in terms of reduced pollution damage, the relevant issue at that point is the extra reduction in damage achieved as a result of reducing emissions by one more unit – the 'Marginal Environmental Damage'.

The key insight from this approach is that the total net benefit to society from pollution control will be maximized (subject to certain qualifications which we can explore later) at the level of

3. The Cambridge economist A. C. Pigou (1877–1959). Pigou's work on the theory of externalities laid the foundations for modern environmental economics. He is now best known for advocating taxes to control externalities

abatement where Marginal Abatement Cost (MAC) and Marginal Environmental Damage (MED) are equal. Suppose that Marginal Abatement Costs rise with increasing pollution control, which will naturally be the case if we do the cheapest things first. (For the moment, let us also assume that Marginal Environmental Damage is constant for each unit of pollution, in other words that each tonne of pollutant causes the same amount of harm.) Then, the first tonne of pollution abatement is socially desirable if the benefit (in terms of avoided MED) exceeds the cost (MAC). Likewise, the second tonne of abatement, and so on, up until the point where the marginal cost of abatement has risen to equal the marginal environmental damage. Before we reach this point, each additional unit of pollution abatement is socially justified in the sense that the additional costs incurred are less than the additional benefits gained, adding to the net gain to society. But pushing pollution abatement beyond the point where marginal abatement cost and marginal damage cost are equal involves moving into territory where additional units of pollution abatement are increasingly expensive (MAC exceeds MED), meaning that the extra abatement costs outweigh the extra reduction in damage, reducing social welfare as a result. If we ask, how much pollution control is socially justified, we have the economist's answer: up until the point where MAC equals MED, but no further.

It is easy to caricature this perspective as a matter of penny-pinching: on each occasion when something good can be done for the environment, or action taken to prevent environmental harm, along comes the practitioner of the dismal science and says 'This is all very well, but *what will it cost*?' This concern with the balance between costs and benefits is not, however, grounded in an obsession with accountancy, or with minimizing the tax burden; neither does it derive from a confusion between the very different concepts of cost, price, and value. It reflects, instead, the recognition that society's productive resources are limited, and that devoting productive resources to one area of activity reduces potential production in other areas.

For society, the opportunity cost of building a new effluent treatment plant to reduce water pollution might be the improvement to schools or hospitals that could be achieved with the same consumption of public resources, or it might be the additional private consumption that people could enjoy if the money saved by not building the treatment plant was returned in lower taxes. The principle that pollution abatement – or more generally, environmental improvement – should be undertaken up to, but not beyond, the point where the cost of the next unit exactly equals the benefit achieved in return is simply a reflection of the principle that if productive resources are used in one activity they should achieve at least as much of value as they would if used for other purposes.

## A useful diagram

Economists frequently use diagrams to illustrate and explain, and the analysis of the previous section can be represented particularly effectively using a simple diagram – the simplest possible version of the 'core' diagram in environmental economics (Figure 4). Readers who prefer may skip this section without losing the thread of the argument. But the diagram helps clarify certain points with more precision than is possible in the verbal exposition.

The diagram shows how abatement costs and the costs of environmental damage vary with the level of emissions. The level of emissions is shown on the horizontal axis (in terms, for example, of tonnes of pollutant emitted), and the emissions level in the absence of any regulation shown as $E_0$. Leftward movements from $E_0$ represent abatement (reductions in emissions).

The two schedules shown on the diagram represent, respectively, the marginal costs of pollution abatement (MAC) and the costs of marginal environmental damage (MED) that would be avoided as a result of one more unit of abatement. In the case of both of these schedules, the height at a particular point shows the marginal cost at that point.

The diagram has been drawn showing the marginal abatement cost to increase with increasing levels of abatement. This is actually quite critical to the argument; but it is also quite plausible, if abatement technologies are being selected by efficient business managers with a concern for costs and profit. Marginal abatement costs will indeed rise with increasing levels of abatement if decisions are made by ranking the abatement cost options in terms

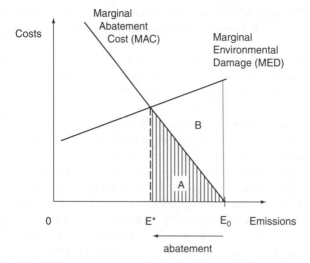

**4. Efficient regulation of an externality balances the costs and benefits of additional pollution abatement**

of abatement cost per tonne, and then implementing the cheapest combination to achieve the required abatement outcome. Also, the marginal environmental damage schedule is shown as smoothly increasing with increasing levels of pollution, and this again is needed if our test for the maximum net benefit to society is always to correctly identify the social optimum. Some environmental problems do not have this increasing relationship between emissions and marginal damage, and the analysis in these cases might need to be more complex.

The level of pollution abatement that maximizes the net benefit to society appears as the point of intersection between the MAC and MED schedules. At this point, identified as the emissions level E* in the diagram, the gain (environmental benefit) from one more unit of pollution abatement is equal to the additional abatement cost (that is, MAC = MED). To the left of this point, MAC exceeds

MED, and additional abatement is more costly to achieve than the environmental benefits it brings. Points to the right of $E^*$ (which involve less abatement than $E^*$) are likewise less desirable than $E^*$; while there is some saving in abatement cost, this is at the expense of an increase in environmental damage that exceeds the abatement cost saving.

One useful feature of this diagram is that it is also possible to identify areas on the diagram which correspond to the total abatement costs incurred in cutting emissions from $E_0$ to $E^*$, and the total benefit obtained, in terms of reduced environmental damage. In each case, the area under the relevant marginal schedule represents the corresponding change in total costs for the overall change in emissions. The total abatement costs incurred in reducing emissions to $E^*$ from the unregulated level $E_0$ is the triangular area marked A on the diagram, and the total environmental benefit from this abatement is the sum of areas A and B (that is, the area under the MED schedule over the range from $E_0$ to $E^*$). The total net benefit to society from this abatement is the difference between these two amounts – in other words the area B. The diagram thus provides a clear visual illustration of the social gains from achieving the optimal level of abatement.

## Yes, but is it fair?

The economic perspective on the regulation of pollution and other forms of environmental protection regulation differs sharply from other approaches – both those that focus simply on the environment and those that focus on individual rights or fairness.

The economic criterion for the level of resources to be devoted to pollution abatement considers matters in terms of abatement costs and environmental benefits, without considering how these are distributed across society. Very often, the abatement costs and environmental benefits will accrue to different individuals.

Reducing emissions may require abatement spending by polluting firms, while the gains from reduced air pollution might be felt by others – by citizens whose health would otherwise have been harmed, by public authorities that might have needed to spend resources cleaning the damaged façades of historic buildings, by other firms which would otherwise have had to install costly air filters to prevent their delicate production processes being harmed by airborne dirt and chemicals, and so on. It seems like the guilty – the polluters – are being asked to spend money reducing the harm they cause to their innocent victims – surely a matter of self-evident justice? So why stop at MAC = MED? Why not demand that the polluters spend more on clean-up, and reduce their emissions wherever this would benefit their innocent victims?

The economist could make three points in reply.

First, the illustration is too convenient, and just happens to slant the pattern of costs and benefits in a way which aligns reassuringly with the pattern of guilt and innocence. Not all polluters are impersonal commercial enterprises, recklessly harming private citizens in the pursuit of profit. Indeed, the consumers of goods that are produced by polluters are, in a sense, contributors to the environmental harm through their consumption decisions. We may all be polluters as well as victims of pollution. To some extent, too, we all bear the costs of abatement measures. The costs of pollution abatement will feed through into product prices; the more we as a society ask polluters in industry X to curb their pollution, the higher will be the prices we pay for its products. For example, the prices of carbon-intensive products may have to rise to reflect the cost of abating the harm to the global climate that their production causes (and price-induced cuts in consumption will be a key mechanism to reduce our 'carbon footprint'). Thinking of abatement in these terms naturally focuses the question on the total costs and benefits; what do we collectively gain in terms of environmental benefits for the costs we will collectively incur?

Second, the criterion is not *intended* to fix problems of social justice, or to define a socially just outcome. It simply defines the 'efficient' level of abatement expenditure, in the specific sense that economists use the concept of efficiency – in other words, the level of spending that achieves the maximum *total net benefit* from the resources used. Suppose the problem is one where the workshops of the poor pollute the pleasure-grounds of the rich; it will still be the case that we can define an efficient level of abatement, in which the abatement costs incurred by polluters are more-than-covered by the benefits achieved, but in this case we would be far less comfortable placing the burden of clean-up on 'guilty' polluters. The question of the fair distribution of costs and benefits is one that we may wish to approach separately, and in the light of the overall pattern of income and wealth in society, and not just the distribution of gains from environmental policies.

Third, the economist would argue that environmental principles that do not consider cost are ultimately unhelpful in addressing some of the most pressing and difficult environmental issues that society faces. If all human life and economic activity involves some degree of environmental damage, we may be unable to eliminate all pollution and environmental harm without shutting down all productive activity. As a guide to practical action, therefore, we need some criterion by which to judge the level of economic sacrifice that we would be willing to incur across other areas of human activity, in order to avoid unacceptable levels of environmental harm. Other ways of balancing costs and benefit can of course be considered, but we cannot escape the need to draw the line somewhere.

This is not in any way to deny the significance of issues of social justice in general, or in relation to environmental policy. Some of the most important, in practice, concern the balance of interests between rich and poor. Some environmental problems, at least, impose particular burdens on the poor, and poorer neighbourhoods tend to be more polluted than the places where better-off households live. Much of the reason for this is that the rich can afford to move to more affluent, cleaner neighbourhoods, and, if we accept that we have to have factories, or power plants, or landfill sites, or incinerators, the likelihood is that the people who are willing to live in their vicinity will be those without the money to go elsewhere. To a large extent the problem is one of poverty in general, rather than environmental poverty specifically, and the remedies may be as much to do with the overall distribution of income as with the pro-poor targeting of environmental improvements.

## Coase's counter-argument

But have we already taken a step too far in claiming to have established the economic basis for environmental regulation? In a radical paper, 'The Problem of Social Cost', published at the start of the 1960s, Ronald Coase challenged the conventional wisdom that pollution problems require regulatory intervention by governments. His paper made the startling claim that, in certain conditions, pollution problems and other externalities could be fully rectified through individual bargaining between the parties involved, without the need for any government policy intervention at all.

What has become known as the Coase Theorem sets out the conditions under which bargaining between a polluter and the victims of pollution could achieve the socially desirable level of pollution abatement, as the outcome of entirely voluntary negotiation. What is more, Coase argued that this could be achieved, regardless of how the law allocates rights between polluters and those affected by their pollution. The law might place no constraints on pollution, or alternatively it might give citizens the legally enforceable right to insist, if they wish, on zero pollution. Either way, Coase argued, these allocations of legal rights simply define the starting point for possible negotiation between polluters and their victims that may be able to achieve a better outcome, for both parties, than the initial starting point.

In a situation of voluntary negotiation, both parties will only consent to deals that represent an improvement against their starting position. Where the polluter faces no legal restriction, the victim would need to offer a payment to induce the polluter to cut their emissions, since otherwise the polluter would have no reason to agree. However, if the damage suffered by the victim is high, the victim might indeed be willing to offer such a payment, and if the abatement costs of the polluter are low, this payment might also be acceptable to the polluter. If both parties pursue the negotiation to find the best possible deal, Coase argued that the outcome would coincide exactly with the social optimum we defined earlier, in which the externality would be cut back to the point where the marginal abatement cost equals the cost of marginal environmental damage.

By a symmetrical argument, there would be potential for mutually beneficial negotiation from the starting point where citizens have the right not to be exposed to harm from a pollution externality. In this case, the polluter would clearly need to pay the victim to accept some level of pollution exposure. Such a deal might be acceptable to both parties, however, if abatement is costly relative to the costs of pollution damage.

According to Coase and his followers, this argument cuts the heart out of the economic case for policy action to regulate pollution and other problems involving externalities. If bargaining between individual firms and citizens can adequately resolve problems of pollution externalities, then environmental regulation is pointless. What then really matters is that the law should define a clear starting point for negotiation, in the form of an unambiguous initial assignment of rights, and then uphold the outcome of any subsequent bargaining.

In practice, it seems clear that the conditions required for successful 'Coasean' bargaining drastically limit its usefulness as a solution to the problem of pollution regulation. First, and most obviously, the process of bargaining itself involves costs. Where many people are involved, either polluters or 'victims', these costs will rise, and negotiating a deal that is acceptable to everyone will inevitably be more complex. Successful bargaining between a polluter and local residents is also likely to be undermined by the systematic weakness in voluntary collective action known as 'free-riding'. Individuals will be reluctant to contribute to the cost of any agreement, reasoning that they can save their own money, while still benefiting from whatever deal is struck without their participation. A further obstacle to a successful bargaining outcome is that the parties may be poorly informed about the interests of the other side and the constraints on their ability to reach a deal. Negotiation may fail, not because there is in principle no mutually beneficial deal available, but because one or other party is sufficiently misinformed about the interests of the other party that they make unrealistic demands.

So, all in all, Coase's analysis seems much more exciting as a theoretical exercise than as a practical approach to environmental policy. There remains one area of policy, however, where bargaining between affected parties has, perforce, to take centre stage. This is the case of international environmental policy problems, where countries' actions – to pollute or to control pollution – affect the interests of other countries. Without an international authority able to coerce countries into taking action, all national actions on international environmental problems are essentially undertaken voluntarily – as the outcome of some form of negotiated agreement which each sovereign country has the right to accept or reject. Coase's analysis provides the foundations for an analytical framework for thinking about this process – and grounds for guarded optimism that in some conditions it could achieve satisfactory outcomes.

## Case study: acid rain control

The development of acid rain policies in Europe in the 1980s and 1990s illustrates how the analytical approach described in this chapter can be used to think about aspects of real-world environmental policy. Much of European acid rain policy is now a matter of history rather than current policy controversy, since actions taken two decades ago have sharply reduced the scale of man-made acid rain pollution in Europe. Nevertheless, looking at the example set by European acid rain policy provides lessons and insights for today's policy debates, in particular about climate change.

Acid rain pollution became a major political issue from the 1980s, given particular impetus by the abrupt appearance of Green parties on the political landscape in Germany and some other European countries. Public concern focused on the very visible deterioration of Europe's forests, with dead trees standing as clear evidence of a potent but invisible source of harm. In urban areas too, the consequences of acid rain were all too apparent, etched deeply into the stonework of buildings – including many of Europe's most historic monuments.

Some acidity in rainfall occurs naturally. However, sulphur dioxide and nitrogen oxides emissions from industrial processes had greatly increased the acidity of rainfall in many parts of Europe. The greatest single source was power station emissions of sulphur dioxide, especially from coal-fired power stations burning the high-sulphur brown coal (lignite) which is widely available in much of Europe. The sulphur in the fuel is turned by combustion into emissions of sulphur dioxide ($so_2$), which in the atmosphere then combines with water vapour to form sulphuric acid, which in the end falls as acid rain.

Power stations accounted for almost three-quarters of Europe's sulphur dioxide emissions, and about half of the remainder was

**5. Acid rain damage to the façade of Reims cathedral**

contributed by other large industrial combustion plants – furnaces, retorts, and the like. These sources became the focus of European acid rain policy, because tackling a limited number of the most-polluting power stations had the potential for rapid and significant improvement. Policies to reduce emissions of nitrogen oxides, which also contribute to acid rain, took longer to develop, because emissions arise from a much wider range of sources – including motor vehicles as well as power stations and industrial plants.

Before the 1980s, policies to control acid rain pollution in urban areas had centred on building tall chimneys to disperse emissions high into the atmosphere. These had the result of turning what had been predominantly issues of local environmental protection into significant diplomatic issues, as winds carried emissions hundreds of kilometres from the original source, before depositing them as acid rain well away from the country of origin. Much of the acid rain in Scandinavia, for example, originated in other countries – including power stations in Poland, Germany, and the UK. Recognition of the significance of these cross-boundary effects led in the 1980s to the start of international negotiations over coordinated policy measures to cut sulphur dioxide emissions.

The technological possibilities for abatement of power station $SO_2$ emissions include three broad groups. First, substantial reductions in emissions could be achieved at relatively low cost per tonne by switching to input fuels containing less sulphur. Second, new power stations could be constructed using cleaner combustion technologies, capable of producing more electricity for a given level of input fuel. Third, emissions could be reduced by 'end-of-pipe' effluent cleaning, to filter out the sulphur that power stations would otherwise discharge into the atmosphere. Flue gas desulphurization (FGD) equipment, or 'scrubbers', a substantial piece of physical infrastructure constructed alongside the power station, can remove 90% or more of the sulphur that would otherwise be discharged. Equipping a power station with FGD scrubbers is, however, a massive capital investment, running in tens of millions of pounds for each plant. It was crucial that major investments in FGD equipment should be targeted wisely, and other cheaper options exploited to the full.

So, how could economics help with these decisions? First, and relatively straightforwardly, the construction of marginal abatement cost schedules can help to identify the most efficient combination of abatement measures to achieve any given reduction in $SO_2$ emissions. Work at the IIASA research centre in Vienna developed estimates of marginal abatement cost schedules for each of the European countries, based on detailed information about the costs and abatement potential of each of the available technologies, given the characteristics of power plants in each country. A key insight is that, even though the same technologies were in principle available to every country, marginal abatement costs varied widely across countries. Those that were heavily reliant on high-sulphur brown coal for electricity generation had much more scope for cheap abatement than those that were already using lower-sulphur input fuels, or had already implemented domestic emission control measures.

The IIASA work on MAC schedules suggested that for most European countries there was a fair amount of abatement that could be done at rather low cost per tonne, but that marginal abatement costs then started to rise quite steeply after a point, as increasingly expensive technologies had to be brought into play. How much abatement could then be justified? In particular, were there any emissions sources causing sufficient harm to warrant incurring abatement costs in the more steeply rising part of the MAC schedule?

The benefits of acid rain abatement – the damage costs avoided – vary depending on local circumstances. Acid deposited in areas of high natural vulnerability, such as the thin and vulnerable soils of Scandinavia, causes greater damage than elsewhere. Acid deposited in densely settled urban areas with a high concentration of buildings and motor vehicles causes greater economic losses through acid damage to physical capital than in less densely settled and developed areas. However, a crucial factor affecting the harm done by a power station's emissions is the direction in which its emissions are carried by the prevailing winds. Understanding the international flows of sulphur pollution was essential if abatement investments were to be targeted to the power stations where they could achieve the greatest benefits.

The international flows were also fundamental to the pattern of national interests in the Europe-wide negotiation. Research by

6. Damage to the natural environment caused by acid rain. An acid-damaged forest in Poland, near the border with the Czech Republic, 1990s

EMEP (the European Monitoring and Evaluation Programme) showed the scale of the international flows of sulphur pollution, as winds carried the pollution hundreds of kilometres from the emission source. Of the UK's 2.9 million tonnes of sulphur dioxide emissions in 1991, only 1.1 million tonnes was deposited in the UK itself, and the rest was widely spread – with, for example, 131,000 tonnes deposited in Scandinavia and 95,000 tonnes deposited in Germany. On average across Europe as a whole, only about one-third of a country's emissions of sulphur dioxide fell within its own borders.

The international dispersion of emissions has the immediate implication that purely national action to tackle the problem of acid rain will be limited and costly. For some countries, particularly larger countries whose own emissions of $SO_2$ fall to a significant extent within their own borders, some national policy action to reduce acid rain damage would be worthwhile, even without any international agreement. Not all European countries, however, had any real prospect of reducing acid rain damage through their own actions. For Scandinavia as a whole, for example, the area's own $SO_2$ emissions accounted for only 22% of the man-made acidity in rainfall, and most originated abroad. International agreement was crucial for the Scandinavian countries. Even if they cut their own $SO_2$ emissions to zero, they could only reduce the sulphur deposition in acid rain by a mere 22%.

For the parts of Europe, like Scandinavia, whose acid rain was largely imported, the need for an international agreement to sulphur dioxide emissions was clear and pressing; without it, their acid rain problem could not be solved. But even those countries where imported acid was less significant would stand to gain from other countries' actions to reduce emissions. On average across Europe as a whole, these cross-country spillover effects from each individual country's abatement are about of the same order of magnitude as the purely domestic benefits. As a result, in any cost–

Table 1. National emissions of sulphur dioxide in 1991, and where they were deposited

| | Deposition of $SO_2$ 1000s of tonnes | Percentage of deposition from own emission sources | Emissions of $SO_2$ 1000s of tonnes | Percentage of emissions deposited domestically |
|---|---|---|---|---|
| UK | 1232 | 85% | 2906 | 36% |
| Germany | 2700 | 72% | 4705 | 41% |
| Scandinavia | 1151 | 22% | 604 | 42% |
| Other Western Europe | 4171 | 59% | 4741 | 52% |
| Former USSR | 6446 | 58% | 4763 | 79% |
| Eastern Europe | 6707 | 70% | 7628 | 62% |
| Known sea deposition | 7341 | | | |
| Other/ unknown | 804 | | 5404 | |
| Total | 30751 | | 30751 | |

Source: Hilde Sandnes (1993) Country to Country Deposition Budget Matrices, EMEP/MSC–W Report 1/92

Note: The data understate the overall significance of cross-country acid rain deposition, because the percentages shown for each group of countries do not include the cross-country deposition within each group.

benefit test of abatement measures, a significantly higher level of abatement is likely to be justified if Europe-wide benefits are taken into account, than if the measures are judged solely in terms of the environmental benefits within a country that result from its own abatement actions.

This is the core of the case for international policy agreements on acid rain, global climate change, and other environmental problems where the environmental effects spread beyond national boundaries. More can be achieved through coordinated action than would be achieved if each country looked only at the domestic benefits that arise from its own abatement actions. This is not an appeal to altruism (although there may be international environmental problems where altruistic action by rich countries may be right and proper). Instead, the logic is more a matter of 'you scratch my back and I'll scratch yours'. Countries that do more abatement than is justified in terms of national environmental improvement confer benefits elsewhere, and at the same time benefit from lower imports of acid rain as a result of the policy actions taken elsewhere.

The problem for acid rain policy, however, was that the benefits from coordinated action would be very unevenly distributed. Windflows across Europe do not spread emissions uniformly; instead there are prevailing winds which tend to mean that some countries may export much more acid rain to other countries in Europe than they import in return. Because the prevailing winds are from the south-west, the UK and Ireland, for example, contributed more acid rain to the rest of Europe than they received in return.

Drawing together these observations about the possibilities and costs of abatement and the level and distribution of environmental damage the Swedish economist Karl-Göran Mäler studied the pattern of national interests in the Europe-wide negotiations over acid rain control. In his hugely influential 1991 paper 'The Acid Rain Game', he showed the nature of the strategic interactions between countries, and the fundamental problem that some countries stood to lose quite significantly from participating in an agreement that would maximize Europe-wide benefits. Because of the pattern of prevailing winds, the UK would need to cut emissions by considerably more than many other countries, while benefiting much less than average in terms of reduced acid imports. Why on earth would a country in this position sign the agreement – a voluntary act that makes them worse-off than if there were no deal? Unsurprisingly, the UK chose not to participate in the first European agreement on acid rain, the first Sulphur Protocol, signed in 1985.

Mäler observed that there was in principle a simple solution to this otherwise fatal obstacle to agreement. If there are indeed overall benefits for Europe as a whole from the deal, then the countries that gain will gain by more than enough to be able to compensate the countries that lose. By making compensation payments between countries it will therefore be possible to redistribute the overall gains so that no participant loses. Economists refer to such payments as side-payments. In principle, they provide a complete and neat solution to the problem that what may collectively benefit a group of countries as a whole may not directly benefit every single member of the group.

Like many neat solutions, however, practical application is far from straightforward. Side payments formed no part of the European agreements on acid rain. Nor have they been widespread features of other international environmental negotiations. The fundamental obstacle is a political one: How many politicians could sell an international agreement to their domestic public, if a key component was that the countries harmed by international pollution had to make large cash payments to those who caused the problem?

If this is an insuperable obstacle, there are two alternatives. One is somehow to conceal the side payments, perhaps by linking agreement to other negotiations in which the flows of costs and benefits coincidentally happen in the opposite direction. The UK did sign up to the second Sulphur Protocol, agreed in 1994, possibly because the diplomatic damage that would have been caused by its continuing refusal would have exceeded the costs of participation. The other option is to constrain the pattern of obligations in international agreements to those which ensure that no individual participant is a net loser. This may significantly undermine the overall benefits of the agreement in some cases, and in other cases may be a fatal obstacle to any agreement at all.

So we end with a somewhat pessimistic conclusion. There will be many obstacles to securing international agreement on comprehensive measures to control environmental problems which cross national boundaries. An efficient agreement which takes account of both abatement costs and the pattern of environmental benefits may require different countries to contribute very different amounts of abatement; this may well seem inequitable, and so agreement may be difficult to reach. Some of the most difficult obstacles to agreement arise where the effects of pollution – and consequently the benefits of abatement – are unevenly distributed. It is an uncomfortable fact of diplomatic life that in this situation no deal is likely unless the 'victims' of the pollution finance a significant part of the abatement costs incurred by the polluters.

# Chapter 3
# Environmental policy: instrument choice

Walk down any UK high street, and the stream of shoppers coming towards you will be carrying their shopping in distinctive plastic carrier bags – orange from Sainsbury's, green from Marks and Spencer, white and biodegradable from the Co-op. Walk down the major shopping streets in Dublin, in the Irish Republic, however, and it is far harder to guess where people have been shopping. You'll see a diverse mixture of bags – many unbranded and more durable than the flimsy plastic bags provided by UK supermarkets, and others clearly re-used from earlier shopping trips.

The difference can be traced to a tax. In 2002, the Irish government introduced a 15 cent tax on plastic shopping bags, which had previously been provided free by supermarkets to their customers. The aim was to stop the environmental eyesore of discarded bags littering the countryside, and the wasteful and unnecessary use of resources. The tax had widespread public support – indeed the Irish economist Frank Convery thinks it may be the most popular tax in Europe. And it had a dramatic effect, cutting the number of plastic carrier bags used by 90% almost overnight. It is a change, also, that has been sustained. The 15 cents levy is enough to discourage stores from handing out unlimited bags for free, and where they have passed on the tax by charging their customers for each bag taken, this has been enough to encourage many shoppers to bring their own bags.

The Irish plastic bags levy is just one illustration of the way in which governments have begun to use taxes and other incentive-based policies to encourage 'green' behaviour. The last two decades have seen an explosion of interest in the scope for using incentive-based environmental policies – so-called 'market mechanisms' – including taxes on landfill sites, air travel, polluting batteries, pesticides, carbon-based energy sources, and on various polluting emissions from industry, tax reductions for cleaner motor fuels, cleaner vehicles, and energy-saving materials, emissions trading schemes for sulphur dioxide, landfill capacity, and carbon dioxide, and many more.

Economists have been enthusiastic advocates of this approach, both as a way of finding solutions to some of the new environmental problems being encountered, and also as a potential improvement on older approaches to environmental regulation. Conventional 'command and control' regulation of industrial pollution, for example, which requires polluters to use certain types of pollution control equipment or sets limits on their polluting emissions, has led to enormous improvements in many environmental problems over recent decades. But advocates of market mechanisms have argued that conventional regulation has been unduly costly and inflexible, and that incentive-based approaches, for example using environmental taxes or emissions trading, have some significant advantages. The relative merits of these two approaches to environmental policy have been the focus of intensive debate over the last two decades, both in academic and policy circles.

Shoppers' behaviour, in the face of the Irish plastic bag tax, illustrates one of the main issues at stake. An even greater reduction in the use of plastic carrier bags could have been achieved by the simple expedient of a law banning their use outright. But this would have imposed very high costs in terms of inconvenience on some shoppers. While many shoppers can easily bring enough old bags and re-usable bags to hold their groceries, those buying larger amounts than usual, or having to make unexpected shopping trips, or those simply forgetful or improvident would find a complete ban very inconvenient. The 15 cent levy provides a neat way of encouraging shoppers not to take plastic bags when they are able to use an alternative or can carry their purchases away without a bag at all, while at the same time providing a safety valve for those finding themselves making purchases without any available bags. The idea that prices provide flexibility, encouraging behavioural changes when these can be made relatively cheaply, while not compelling everyone to do the same, is central to the argument for using market mechanisms in environmental policy.

## 'Command and control' environmental regulation

The conventional approach to environmental regulation, rather pejoratively referred to as 'command-and-control', typically uses laws or other regulatory processes to require changes in polluters' behaviour. The regulation can take a number of forms:

- Firms may be required to make use of particular pollution-abatement technologies. For example, in most European countries, the acid rain legislation which implemented the requirements of the EU's Large Combustion Plant Directive mandated the installation of FGD scrubbers in new power stations, and required FGD technology to be retrofitted to some existing power stations.
- Limits can be placed on pollutant concentrations in flows of effluent discharges. For example, waste water discharges from an industrial facility might be limited to no more than X parts per million of mercury.
- The regulator may place limits on total effluent emissions from particular sources over a specified time period. For example, the US Environmental Protection Agency's National Pollutant Discharge Elimination System (NPDES) controls polluting emissions of organic and toxic effluents to lakes and

rivers from industrial and municipal sources by issuing permits which typically specify both average monthly discharge limits and maximum daily limits, each specified in terms of the quantity of each pollutant that can be emitted over the relevant time period. Where the maximum daily limits are set higher than the average monthly limit, this allows a limited amount of day-to-day variation in emission levels.

One important consideration in choosing between these various different forms of regulation would be the nature of the impact on the environment. For example, monthly or annual limits make more sense when pollution damage depends on the total amount of emissions that accumulate in the environment over this time period, and less sense if environmental damage varies from day to day according to daily variations in emissions.

The enforcement of compliance is another important issue. If regulations require the installation of particular technologies, a simple inspection visit may suffice to check whether individual firms have the required equipment in place. Checking that the equipment is switched on (yes!) and working to full efficiency cannot be verified so quickly and cheaply, and if it is costly to run the equipment – and therefore temptingly profitable to switch it off – more frequent inspection visits may be needed. Where command-and-control regulation sets limits on pollutant concentrations in effluent flows, it may be possible to achieve a good level of compliance through occasional, unannounced checks on pollutant levels, so long as these are backed up with sufficiently severe sanctions for those plants found to be exceeding the limits set. On the other hand, a limit on total monthly or annual emissions may require a completely different approach to monitoring, based on continuous measurement of emission levels. Continuous recording of effluent flows through a chimney or discharge pipe has in the past been costly and difficult, but recent technological advances may be widening the scope for this approach.

The regulator's costs and convenience should not be the only considerations in the design of regulation. Equally important, from the social point of view, are the costs incurred by the firms subject to regulation, including the abatement costs required to meet the requirements of the regulation, and the compliance costs incurred in dealing with whatever arrangements are in place for monitoring and enforcement. Capital and labour resources used for these activities, just like the resources used by the government in regulation, have an opportunity cost, in the form of the valuable goods and services that they could otherwise produce. The next section will discuss the reasons to believe that abatement costs will be lower, for a given level of environmental quality, if market mechanisms are employed rather than conventional command and control regulation. Whether monitoring and compliance costs for firms are lower with one approach or the other is far less clear. But at all events, the authorities will need to undertake enforcement and monitoring activities with environmental policies of all sorts – it is not enough to pass laws and simply trust that they will be obeyed – and the costs to firms of complying with these enforcement activities need to be taken into account.

## The case for market mechanisms

Environmental taxes and emissions trading are the two most prominent and widespread categories of 'economic instruments' (or 'market mechanisms') in environmental policy. What they have in common is that people taking decisions that affect the level of pollution face a financial incentive to reduce emissions. The simplest example is an environmental tax or charge levied directly on each tonne of polluting emissions. With this tax, the polluter pays a 'price' for each tonne emitted, and, as a result, gains from taking action to reduce emissions, through the reduction in tax payments. Similarly with an emissions trading system. If the rules require that polluters have to surrender one emissions allowance for every tonne of pollution, then polluters must pay to obtain the allowances needed for each tonne of pollution, and can save on allowance purchases, or sell their surplus allowances, whenever they take actions to cut emissions.

The distinctive feature of this form of regulation, shared both by the pollution tax and tradeable pollution permits, is that polluting is costly to the polluter – in the sense that they must pay tax or use permits – and this cost creates an incentive for changes in polluting behaviour.

The most straightforward context in which to explore the properties of environmental market mechanisms is the case of the tax or charge on polluting emissions, discussed in this section. Later in the chapter, the analysis is extended to consider the use of emissions trading. In many important respects, emissions trading works in a very similar way to a pollution tax; in other respects it raises new and distinctive issues.

One point is worth making at the outset. The arguments for using market mechanisms rather than conventional 'command and control' regulation are almost entirely independent of the basis on which decisions are made about how much pollution control should be achieved. Whether the target reduction in pollution is set on the basis of an 'efficient' tradeoff between marginal abatement costs and marginal environmental damage, as discussed in Chapter 2, or set on the capricious whim of a politician, or determined on some other basis, does not in itself have any implications for instrument choice. The relative merits of different instruments for pollution control apply (in the main) regardless of how the pollution-control target was set. The one obvious exception is the really rather rare case where the decision has been taken to cut emissions to zero; in this case, an outright ban clearly makes most sense, and there is little merit to thinking about taxes or trading alternatives.

At the core of the economic argument for market mechanisms lie issues of flexibility and incentives. The flexibility offered by

43

## Market mechanisms: some examples

### Emissions taxes and charges

- Charge on emissions of nitrogen oxides by large industrial boilers in Sweden (1992)
- Charges for industrial water pollution in the Netherlands and France
- 'Landfill Taxes' on waste disposal in the UK, Austria, Netherlands, Norway, Belgium, etc.

### Environmental taxes on products

- High taxes on motor fuels (petrol and diesel) reflect environmental costs, congestion, and other externalities
- Tax reductions for unleaded petrol in most European countries in the 1980s and 1990s
- Taxes on batteries in Sweden, Denmark, Belgium, Austria, etc.
- $CO_2$ taxes in Denmark, Norway, Sweden, and Finland
- Plastic bag levy in Ireland (2002)

### Emissions trading / Tradeable permits

- Tradeable permits for industrial effluent discharges to a polluted stretch of the Fox River, Wisconsin (1981)
- US inter-refinery trading in lead-reduction credits (to phase out leaded petrol), 1982–8
- US Acid Rain Program (trading in power station $SO_2$ emissions, started 1995)
- EU Emissions Trading Scheme (for carbon used by power stations and large firms, started 2005)

market mechanisms allows them to achieve any chosen environmental improvement at a lower economic cost to society as a whole. Or alternatively, for a given cost, the use of more flexible mechanisms with lower cost per unit of abatement would make it possible for society to purchase more environmental improvement than with existing regulatory approaches. The economic incentives established by market mechanisms play a key role, as we will see, in achieving the benefits of flexibility. In addition, market mechanisms create incentives for innovations in pollution abatement technologies that hold out the potential for additional environmental improvements in the long run.

These effects operate through rather different processes in the two main groups of market mechanism introduced in environmental policy in recent decades, environmental taxes and emissions trading. However, the underlying principle is the same in both cases. Both place a price on polluting, in the first case by taxing it, in the second through the market price that has to be paid for emissions permits. This price discourages pollution; where abatement is cheaper than the price that has to be paid for polluting, polluters will prefer to undertake abatement. At the same time, the use of pricing rather than rigid and uniform regulation offers flexibility to polluters with very high costs of pollution abatement because they can choose to pay the price, in terms of tax or permit costs, instead of incurring high abatement costs. Pricing pollution thus discourages emissions where abatement is relatively inexpensive, while offering a safety-valve where abatement costs are excessively high. If the price is set at the appropriate level, more cheap abatement will be done than if a uniform regulatory standard applies to all polluters, and fewer expensive abatement measures will be needed, achieving a given total of abatement at lower overall cost.

Economists refer to this outcome as the 'static efficiency' case for market mechanisms: the flexibility achieved by pricing pollution rather than rigid regulation achieves a given outcome at lower overall cost. The cost savings are greater, the larger are the differences in marginal abatement costs between different firms, because there is then a large benefit from reallocating abatement to where it can be done most cheaply. Research on the pattern of abatement costs for various pollution problems suggests considerable potential for cost savings through the use of market mechanisms. According to a range of estimates collected by the US economist Tom Tietenberg the costs of air pollution control in various locations in the US could be anything from 1.07 times to 22 times more costly with uniform command-and-control regulations than using market mechanisms which achieve the least-cost abatement outcome. On average across these studies, efficient allocation of abatement could achieve the same environmental quality as uniform command-and-control, at only one-sixth of the cost.

Almost certainly, however, these estimates overstate the potential gains. Command-and-control policies usually manage to differentiate to some extent between firms with high and low abatement costs, for example, by imposing higher requirements on new plants than on existing plants (where abatement would usually be more costly), though this can slow the rate at which new, clean firms replace old dirty ones. And while market mechanisms may work better than command and control, they are unlikely to be able to achieve all potential efficiency gains.

Much will depend in practice on the way in which polluters respond to the incentives provided by pollution taxes or emissions trading. To realize the potential gains in efficiency which in principle are offered by market mechanisms could require polluters to rethink their business decision-making processes quite radically. Efficient business decisions would require firms to bring together production engineering and technology information about abatement options and costs, to compare with the savings that can be made in reduced tax or permit purchases. The existing organizational structure of firms may not always be

7. The UK's Landfill Tax, introduced in 1996, is paid on each tonne of waste dumped at landfill sites, with the aim of encouraging local authorities and businesses to seek alternative forms of waste disposal, to make more use of recycling, and to reduce waste generation

well-suited to deal with such issues: taxation may, for example, be treated simply as a matter of accountancy, and the accountants may simply pay any tax bills due without ever bringing them to the attention of the firm's pollution-control engineers. Efficient responses to market mechanisms may therefore require adaptations in the internal organization and behaviour of businesses. These changes may be costly to make, and are more likely to be prompted by high-profile policy instruments, imposing large costs, than by small taxes, for example, which may not make the organizational adjustment worthwhile.

At heart, the case for market mechanisms is an argument about the limitations on regulatory capacity, with close echoes of more general arguments about the limitations of central planning, as opposed to markets, as a way of organizing economic activity. It is clear that an all-knowing, all-powerful environmental regulator could achieve an environmental outcome just as good as any that could be achieved through market mechanisms, by taking account of the differences in abatement costs and opportunities of different polluters, and issuing appropriately differentiated regulatory instructions. But real-world regulators face problems in obtaining information, and in getting people to do what they want.

Much of the information about the pattern of abatement costs that the regulator would need in order to identify the cheapest way to achieve a given total abatement is in the hands of polluters themselves. Where the polluters are industrial firms, for example, it concerns details of their production activity, organization, and costs. It is not in the interests of polluters to provide the regulator with information about these costs. Quite apart from the fact that this may often be sensitive commercial information, individual polluters would be only too well aware of the implications of the information they provide. Those with lower abatement costs than the average could anticipate that if they reveal the true position to the regulator they will be asked to do more abatement than others. For some polluters, it is better to keep the regulator in a position of ignorance, or worse still, to mislead the regulator about their true abatement costs, in order to avoid the demands for pollution abatement that they would otherwise face. The problem of informed regulation is not just one of processing the large volume of information, but of getting hold of it in the first place.

By contrast, market mechanisms achieve the least-cost abatement outcome with very low requirements for information. The regulator does not need to know the abatement costs of each individual firm, but instead sets the price for emissions (either by setting the tax rate, or by setting the emissions cap which leads to a permit price), and polluters then self-select so that those with lower abatement costs do more abatement than those for whom abatement costs are higher. Given that the price applies uniformly to all firms, there is no reason for them to do otherwise.

True, to set environmental policy efficiently, the regulator does need to know about overall marginal abatement costs, if the level of abatement at which MAC = MED is to be identified. But this is much less demanding than knowing the individual costs of each and every firm. In practice, most estimates of industry-level marginal abatement cost schedules are built up from a knowledge of the range of abatement technologies available in the industry and the rough proportion of firms to which each would be applicable, without any attempt to identify the costs of individual firms. And even if the overall marginal abatement costs schedule is not known with complete accuracy, it will still be the case that the flexibility of market mechanisms saves on costs of achieving the abatement outcome.

In addition to the cost savings in achieving abatement through efficient deployment of current abatement technologies, market mechanisms offer a further set of potential gains, in terms of their long-term encouragement to innovation in abatement technology. With market mechanisms, polluters face a continuing incentive for pollution-reducing innovation. The incentive arises because, even after taking all cost-effective abatement measures, polluters face a cost for each unit of residual pollution, in the form of the environmental tax on each unit of emissions, payments for the allowances needed to cover their remaining emissions, or forgone revenue from the sale of permits that would be 'freed-up' through additional abatement. This creates an incentive to innovate, and develop new cost-effective abatement methods, since these can further reduce the firm's outlay on pollution taxes or permits. Typically, with 'command-and-control' regulation, in which firms are required to make specified abatement investments, or observe a quantitative limit of emissions, this innovation incentive is absent, because the firm has no reason to go beyond compliance with the requirements of the regulation. In the long run, therefore, regulation through market mechanism would be expected to encourage the development and commercialization of new pollution control technologies more rapidly (and with a greater focus on cost-effective technologies) than under traditional command-and-control regulation.

## Designing and implementing eco-taxes

The simplest form of environmental tax, in theory, although rarely encountered in practice, would be a tax based directly on measured emissions from each source. The owner of a polluting factory would receive a quarterly or annual bill for pollution, based on the factory's actual emissions in the period, in kilograms of pollutant, multiplied by a charge per kilogram. Pollution taxes would then closely resemble electricity bills, or bills for metered water use. One well-established example of this approach is the tax on nitrogen oxides emissions in Sweden.

Environmental taxes based directly on measured emissions can, in principle, be very precisely targeted to the policy's environmental objectives. If a firm pollutes more, it pays additional tax directly in proportion to the rise in emissions. The polluter thus has an incentive to reduce emissions in any manner that is less costly per unit of abatement than the tax on each unit of residual emissions. The great attraction of basing the tax directly on measured emissions is that the actions the polluter can take to reduce tax liability are actions that also reduce emissions. Continuous emissions measurement can be costly, particularly where there are many separate sources of emissions, and for many pollution problems this may be a major deterrent to direct taxation of emissions. Nevertheless, the technologies available for monitoring the concentrations and flows of particular substances in effluent discharges have been developing rapidly. In the future, it may be possible to think of taxing measured emissions in a wider range of applications.

In practice, however, most existing environmentally related taxes are not based on directly measured emissions, but are levied on the sale of commodities that are related to emissions or pollution. For example, the sale of motor fuel is taxed heavily, in the belief that raising its price will encourage changes in behaviour that will reduce motor vehicle emissions. Sometimes products believed to benefit the environment may be taxed less heavily than their substitutes, as with reduced tax on lead-free petrol.

Restructuring the existing tax system along these lines can be a relatively straightforward way of introducing fiscal incentives to reduce environmental damage, without the need to incur the costs of monitoring and measuring actual emissions. Adapting and extending the existing mechanisms for taxing transactions may be a cheaper alternative.

The risk with this approach, however, is that the incentive may be too poorly targeted to achieve the desired environmental outcome. In a pioneering discussion of the economic issues in environmental taxation, the Norwegian economist Agnar Sandmo described an experiment in some Norwegian communities which

## The tax on nitrogen oxides emissions in Sweden

The nitrogen oxides (NOx) charge in Sweden, introduced in 1992 as part of Sweden's programme of measures to reduce acid rain, is an example of an environmental tax based directly on measured emissions. It is levied on measured NOx emissions, at a rate of SKr 40 per equivalent kilogram of nitrogen dioxide (about £4000 per tonne).

The tax only applies to a small group of large industrial boilers and power plants. The cost of emissions measurement at each plant is high – around SKr 300,000 (some £30,000) annually per plant – and only worthwhile for large plants, where the gains from more efficient abatement can outweigh the measurement costs. The charge applies to plants with an energy output of at least 25 GWh/year – about 260 plants in total, accounting for around half the total NOx emissions from industrial power generation in Sweden.

To avoid distorting competition between the large plants subject to the NOx charge and their smaller competitors, almost all of the revenues are returned to the participating firms, in proportion to the amount of energy they produce. Plants with high emissions relative to their energy output are net payers to the scheme, while plants with low emissions relative to energy output are net recipients. The tax raises no net revenues; its sole purpose is to incentivize more efficient abatement of NOx emissions.

tried to charge for household waste collection and disposal by charging for the black plastic sacks which households were required to use. Many US communities have tried similar approaches, either charging for sacks, or for special stickers to be placed on each garbage sack put out for collection. The evidence is that these approaches do reduce household waste generation (particularly when accompanied by good facilities for recycling), but they also induce changes in behaviour which do not reduce waste quantities. For example, households may try to economize on the expensive sacks or stickers by cramming much more into each sack than they did before – a phenomenon sometimes dubbed the 'Seattle stomp'! As Sandmo points out, this is a natural consequence of the poor targeting of the incentive, charging for the sacks, rather than for the waste itself. More generally, taxing transactions may be straightforward, but will not target the incentives for environmental improvement as accurately as can be achieved when measured emissions are taxed directly.

The last two decades have seen considerable excitement in policy circles about the possibility that large revenues could be generated from environmental taxes, sufficient to finance major tax reform. Quite a number of the environmental taxes that countries have introduced have been accompanied by very explicit measures to reduce the burden of other taxes. So, for example, revenues from the UK's Landfill Tax, introduced in 1996, were almost entirely returned to taxpayers through a reduction in employer's National Insurance Contributions (a payroll tax, based on employee wages). In Sweden, the revenues from a carbon tax, introduced in 1991, were used to finance a reduction in income tax rates. In both cases, a very clear link was drawn between the environmental tax and the tax cuts made elsewhere. This highlighted the environmental purpose of the tax, and helped to secure public acceptance more readily, by countering the suspicion that this was yet another ruse by government to raise the overall tax burden.

Some, however, have argued for a large-scale 'green tax reform', in which the tax system would be rebalanced, to 'tax bads, not goods' – in other words to increase taxation on 'bad' things like pollution, and allow corresponding reductions in existing taxes on 'good' things such as employment and productive activity. The political resonance of these ideas was to an extent strengthened by a rather arcane debate in the economic literature about the potential for such a tax reform to have a 'double dividend', improving the environment, while at the same time securing the government's tax revenues at lower economic cost, by reducing the distortionary and disincentive effects of taxation. This literature generated some unrealistic expectations about the potential economic gains from such a tax shift. But two points are nonetheless clear. First, some environmental tax reforms have the potential to raise significant tax revenues, particularly those that tax energy or carbon at levels that would reflect the scale of environmental risks arising from climate change. Second, it matters a lot what is done with these revenues, and the greatest gains would come from using them in carefully targeted ways to increase the environmental effectiveness of a given level of eco-taxation, or using them to reduce the most distortionary existing taxes.

## The economics of emissions trading

For all the excitement about 'green taxation' and 'eco-tax reform' in policy circles, the two most high-profile and significant market-based innovations in environmental policy in the past two decades have both taken the form of emissions trading schemes, the US Acid Rain Program which began in 1995 and the EU Emissions Trading System for carbon dioxide, introduced a decade later.

In both cases, non-economic factors steered policy-makers in the direction of emissions trading rather than environmental taxation. In the US, President George Bush's 1988 election pledge 'Read My Lips: No New Taxes' compelled policy-makers to look for non-taxation instruments. In the European Union, the rules for decision-making require unanimous agreement among member states on any EU initiatives in the field of taxation, an almost insurmountable hurdle, but only majority agreement on other environmental measures including emissions trading.

In fact, the economic properties of emissions taxes and tradeable emissions permits are remarkably similar. Both depend for their impact on polluters making essentially the same comparison between a financial incentive – the emissions tax per tonne and the emissions permit price per tonne respectively – and firms' marginal abatement cost schedules. This comparison shows the amount of abatement that will be worthwhile, given the size of the financial incentive. If firms face a tradeable permit price of $10 per tonne for emissions, they will choose to abate emissions rather than using permits, whenever the abatement can be done more cheaply than $10 per tonne. Exactly the same calculation would underlie firms' decisions with an emissions tax of $10 per tonne.

In an emissions trading system, permits have value because they are scarce. The system works by issuing fewer permits than the 'business-as-usual' emissions that would occur in the absence of regulation. This limited quantity of permits constrains the total level of emissions, since each tonne of emissions requires the polluter to hold a corresponding permit, and there are not enough to go round. Some polluters therefore are compelled to reduce emissions, by undertaking abatement. The firms that do so will be those that find abatement more attractive than purchasing permits. If the permits can be freely traded, firms will choose abatement if they have relatively low marginal abatement costs; those with higher marginal abatement costs will prefer to use permits instead. The quantity of permits issued thus constrains the overall level of emissions and ensures that sufficient abatement is undertaken to come within this constraint, but trading in the permit market determines the pattern of abatement and emissions across firms.

The market price for permits in an efficiently functioning emissions trading system should settle at the marginal abatement cost for the final unit of abatement needed to meet the emissions constraint set by the quantity of permits issued. The operation

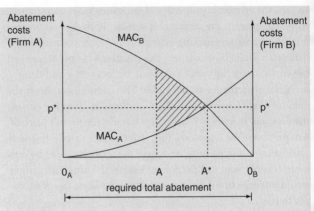

## 8. How emissions trading works: a simple example with two polluters

The diagram represents the range of options for dividing a given abatement requirement between two polluters, A and B. The two polluters face different costs of pollution abatement, with Firm A able to do more low-cost abatement than Firm B. The two firms' marginal abatement cost schedules are represented by $MAC_A$ and $MAC_B$, measured rightwards from the origin $O_A$ and leftwards from the origin $O_B$ respectively. The total costs of abatement will depend on how the total abatement requirement is divided between the two firms, and will be lowest at point $A^*$ where the marginal abatement costs of the two polluters are equal.

At any other point, one firm will have higher marginal abatement costs than the other. If, for example, the initial allocation of permits would require each firm to contribute half the total required abatement (i.e. point A), Firm B has substantially higher marginal abatement costs than Firm A. It would be willing to pay a price up to its marginal abatement cost for an additional permit, while Firm A could reduce its need for permits by one unit by incurring a much lower additional abatement cost. It will be mutually profitable for Firm A to sell an additional permit to Firm B at a price somewhere between the marginal abatement cost of the two firms. By the same logic, assuming a competitive market in permits and no costs of trading, Firm A would profit by increasing abatement to point $A^*$, and selling the permits it no longer needs to Firm B.

The last permit sold by Firm A to Firm B has a value to each of $p^*$, and in a competitive permit market, this is the level at which the permit price would be expected to settle.

The total saving in abatement costs of the two firms from this outcome, compared with a rigid system of regulation which imposes the same abatement requirements on each firm, is given by the shaded area. This will be larger, the greater are the differences in abatement costs between the two firms.

of the market should ensure that abatement is undertaken where it can be done most cheaply (since these are the firms that can profit most from doing abatement rather than using permits). The last unit of abatement needed before the emissions constraint is met will thus be the most costly, and the firm that chooses to undertake it will only do so if the permit price is at least as high as the abatement cost. If the permit price is lower, the firm would buy a permit instead, transferring the requirement for one more unit of abatement to the seller of the permit. But since this abatement will be more costly, the selling firm would not be willing to part with the permit for such a low price. Competition in the market for permits thus ensures that the price settles at the value of the marginal permit used, so that the last permit is held by a polluter who is (very close to) indifferent between holding the permit and undertaking one more unit of abatement.

This process of price determination means that there is a neat symmetry between a well-functioning permit market and a corresponding environmental tax. If an environmental tax set at rate per unit of emissions T leads to an emissions level Q, then alternatively regulating the same problem by issuing a quantity Q of tradeable emissions permits will lead to a permit price per unit of emissions T. Moreover the level and pattern of pollution abatement will be the same under the two instruments, both in total, and its distribution across firms, and the same level of abatement cost will be incurred by the firms. Crucially, both environmental taxes and emissions trading share the key 'static efficiency' property of market mechanisms in environmental policy. Although the institutional mechanisms differ, they both employ price mechanisms to ensure that abatement is undertaken where it can be done most cheaply, thus achieving a given level of abatement at least overall cost.

Substantive differences between environmental taxes and emissions trading do, however, exist, quite apart from the political considerations that attracted US and European legislators to emissions trading as a way of sidestepping the obstacles to taxation. One, of course, is the institutional mechanism of emissions trading itself: for emissions trading to work, the emissions market must function efficiently. The second is that despite the equivalences described above, the two instruments may have rather different properties under conditions of uncertainty. The third is that emissions trading offers a range of options for how permits will be distributed – given away free to existing polluters, or alternatively auctioned to the highest bidder – which raise some interesting political and economic issues.

Real-world emissions trading systems take a number of forms. Some, particularly some of the early schemes, require the regulator to give prior approval for each and every trade, while others allow unrestricted trading subject to later audit of firms' emissions and permit holdings. Some schemes limit trading to transactions between firms in the particular industry that is being regulated, while others allow anyone to buy and sell allowances, opening up the possibility of specialist brokers acting as intermediaries between buyers and sellers. Some allow unused permits to be stored ('banked') for possible use in future periods, while others limit the period of validity of each permit to a single year. These various institutional differences may partly reflect relevant differences in the underlying environmental problem, but they also have important implications for the costs incurred by participants and the overall efficiency with which the market functions.

Various transaction costs might affect the willingness of firms to trade in emission permit markets. These include decision-making costs within the firm (learning how the market works, deciding whether to abate or buy permits), search costs (finding information about market prices, and finding a trading partner), the costs of any negotiation and the transaction itself, and, in some cases, the implicit release of commercially sensitive information to competitors about the firm's abatement technology and costs through the very act of trading itself. The limited research findings on the scale of transactions costs in emissions trading markets suggest that they are non-trivial, especially for smaller and less sophisticated firms, and might reduce the overall achieved gain from trade by perhaps as much as one-third.

Non-competitive behaviour in permit markets could also make them less effective at reallocating abatement to lower-cost sources. This could happen if the initial allocation of allowances concentrates them in a small number of hands, or if the pattern of abatement costs means that only a handful of firms account for nearly all the allowances offered for sale. Where there are too few sellers for the market to be competitive, sellers can make higher profits by limiting the number of allowances offered for sale, in order to obtain a higher price on each allowance sold. As a result, some potential abatement-cost-reducing trades do not take place. Market power outside the allowance market might also affect competition in the allowance market. Firms could, for example, decide to make life hard for their product-market competitors by refusing to sell them pollution permits.

Evidence on the practical significance of market power in emissions trading is sparse. Major emissions trading applications such as the US Acid Rain Program and the EU ETS have a sufficiently large number of potential participants and sufficiently dispersed allowance allocations that problems of market power do not arise. However market power could be an obstacle to efficient functioning of emissions trading in more limited applications. It has, for example, been suggested that this might explain why hardly any trading took place in one of the very early experiments with emissions trading, to regulate the discharges of competing pulp and paper mills on a stretch of the Fox River in Wisconsin.

Ensuring efficient functioning of the permit market is an important issue for regulators considering this approach and the alternative of taxation. However, practical experience shows examples where emission permit markets do indeed function reasonably smoothly, without undue costs for participants or monopoly power. The prospects for emissions trading are best where reasonably large numbers of participants are involved, and trading involves sufficient value that specialist market institutions can develop to provide brokerage and other intermediary services. These tend to reduce transactions costs for unsophisticated participants, and can also maintain market liquidity, making market power less of a risk. Sometimes the way in which market jargon and institutions have developed in emissions trading markets has been seen as evidence that such markets have become subverted by financial interests, and diverted from the proper business of regulating emissions. On the contrary: such institutions play a constructive role in ensuring that emissions trading offers flexibility at low cost to the widest possible range of participants.

A lot of attention has been paid to the differences in the ways in which emissions taxes and emissions trading would be expected to perform under conditions of uncertainty about the technological options and costs of abatement. We have seen that emissions taxes and tradeable emissions permits have very similar properties because they both depend on firms making a similar comparison between their marginal abatement costs and the financial incentive for abatement – the tax per tonne, or the market price of permits per tonne. Given its marginal abatement costs, a firm would react in the same way to either. But there *is* a significant difference in the decision that the regulator has to make with taxes and emissions trading, setting a tax rate in one case and an emissions cap in the other. And if the regulator is very uncertain about abatement costs, it turns out that the consequences of using taxes and emissions trading look very different.

Put simply, if an emissions tax is employed, the regulator sets the tax, but cannot guarantee the abatement outcome; this will depend on the responses of market participants, based on their abatement costs, about which the regulator is uncertain. On the other hand, with emissions trading, the regulator sets a cap on emissions by determining the quantity of permits to be issued; the environmental impact of the regulation is thus guaranteed. On the face of it, the environmental case for using emissions trading when there is uncertainty about abatement costs is clear-cut; emissions trading guarantees a firm cap on emissions while the emissions tax does not.

However, matters are not so simple. The flip-side of the greater certainty about emissions outcomes from trading than with taxes is correspondingly greater uncertainty about abatement costs. Regulation using emissions taxes sets an upper limit on the maximum abatement cost per tonne that firms will incur; this can never exceed the tax per tonne (since firms always have the option of paying the tax instead). With emissions trading, by contrast, the regulator's uncertainty about marginal abatement costs translates into uncertainty about the market price of allowances, and hence the maximum level of abatement costs per tonne that the polluters will face.

Consequently, where the regulator has to set the tax rate or the quantity of permits to be issued, without accurate knowledge of the abatement costs that firms will incur, neither instrument can guarantee that the level of abatement actually achieved will maximize net social gains. Compared with the social optimum (that is, compared with the level of abatement at which true marginal abatement costs equal marginal damage cost) too much abatement, or too little abatement may be undertaken. Moreover, the extent to which the outcome differs from the optimum will generally differ between emissions taxes and tradeable emissions permits. Neither instrument is unambiguously superior when the regulator does not have accurate knowledge of abatement costs. Which is likely to perform better will depend on the relative slopes of the marginal abatement cost and environmental damage schedules (that is, the rates at which marginal abatement costs and marginal pollution damage change when emissions differ from the optimum). Emissions taxes will tend to get closer to the optimal outcome if marginal abatement costs increase with extra abatement more rapidly than marginal environmental damage increases with extra emissions. Emissions trading will perform better if the reverse is true. This is an empirical matter, and will vary from case to case. Some have argued, for example, that it establishes a case for preferring carbon taxes to quantity targets and trading in the control of global climate change, on the grounds that marginal environmental damage is unlikely to be greatly affected by changes in the level of emissions over a period of a few years (since it is the total accumulated stock of carbon dioxide in the atmosphere that matters), while it is possible that marginal abatement costs for carbon dioxide emissions could rise steeply with abatement.

The third area of major difference between environmental taxes and emissions trading is the process by which allowances are distributed. In practice, nearly all emissions trading systems have distributed most or all emissions permits without charge to existing polluters. Typically, polluters would be given an allocation based on some fraction of their emissions in some preceding, 'baseline', year, a process known as 'grandfathering'. Firms would then buy or sell allowances, depending on how their marginal abatement costs compare with the allowance price that emerges in subsequent market trading. The market price will of course be higher, the smaller the total allocation of permits, since the cap on emissions will then be tighter compared with business-as-usual emissions.

As an alternative, emissions trading permits could be auctioned – sold to the highest bidder. Small fractions of allowances in the US Acid Rain Program have been auctioned each year, to ensure that there is at least some liquidity in the market to allow new firms to obtain the permits they need, and a small but increasing fraction of allowances in the EU Emissions Trading System for carbon dioxide is now being sold through auction. The most obvious effect of auctioning is that payments are made for permits, leading to revenues for the government and a corresponding cost for the regulated firms as a whole, who have to pay for allowances that under grandfathering would be distributed for free.

In other respects, auctioning would be expected to make very little difference to the operation of the emissions trading market. The comparisons that firms make in deciding whether to abate and sell permits, or to pollute and buy permits, depend on the same comparison between marginal abatement costs and the permit price. Aside from the possibility that the burden of paying for allowances may induce some firms to leave the market entirely, the permit price would be expected to settle at the same level, regardless of how the permits are distributed. The same firms would then end up holding permits and polluting under either approach, and the same level of abatement would be achieved. The one major difference to the industry would be that firms' profits would be higher under grandfathering than auctioning; essentially because grandfathering distributes valuable assets to firms for free. Views differ as to whether this matters. Some argue that distributing such largesse to polluting firms can buy off potentially fatal industry hostility to tough pollution regulation. Others argue that the value of grandfathered permits is so high that it encourages wasteful lobbying by firms keen to slant the allocation formula in their favour, and risks corruption in the allocation process.

Substantial public revenues could however be raised by auctioning emissions trading permits. For example, if the US Acid Rain Program discussed in the next section were to auction all allowances, this could raise $1 billion or more each year. Choosing to grandfather allowances instead forgoes these revenues, and misses out on the scope to cut existing taxes on labour and capital which impose costly disincentives and distortions on economic behaviour. These distortionary costs could easily add 20 or 30 cents to the total economic burden of every dollar raised through existing taxes, so it is clear that deciding not to auction allowances is a missed opportunity of major economic significance.

## Emissions trading in practice: the US Acid Rain Program

The experience of the US Acid Rain Program, the world's first major application of tradeable pollution permits, demonstrates how emissions trading can be used to facilitate rapid reductions in emissions that would be costly or impracticable with conventional regulation. The legislation which initiated the Acid Rain Program set a permanent cap on the $SO_2$ emissions of US power stations, requiring annual emissions to be cut by 40% within a decade. In parallel, a system of emissions trading in $SO_2$ allowances was introduced, to allow the maximum flexibility in how this cap was reached.

The cap, and the associated emissions trading system, were implemented in two stages. Phase I began in 1995, concentrating on slightly more than a hundred of the dirtiest power stations, located in the east and mid-west, the parts of the country most severely affected by acid rain. Together, this comparatively small group of power stations accounted for about half of the 15.7 million tons of power station $SO_2$ emissions in 1990. Beginning in 1995, the operators of these power stations received annual allocations of emission allowances, declining over time, and were required to turn in allowances corresponding to their $SO_2$ emissions in each year. Operators could choose to use all the allowances they had been allocated, or could reduce their $SO_2$ emissions below their allocation, and keep ('bank') their unused allowances for possible future use, or sell their surplus allowances to other power station operators with emissions in excess of their allowance allocation. During the five years of Phase I, the annual allowance allocation fell from 8.7 million tons in 1995 – the same as actual emissions

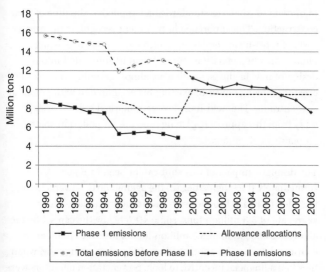

**9. The US Acid Rain Program. Annual allocations of allowances (the emissions cap), and actual emissions from US power stations, 1990–2008**

Source: Author's calculations, based on data from US Environmental Protection Agency, Acid Rain Program Progress Report, various years

from these sources in 1990 – to 7 million tons in 1999, a 20% reduction. Then, in 2000, Phase II extended the emissions cap to all power stations, bringing in many smaller and newer units, some 3,400 operating units in total, and capping their combined emissions at 9.5 million tons annually, 40% below 1990 levels (Figure 9).

The Acid Rain Program demonstrates how it is possible to go further and faster in reducing emissions when the flexibility offered by market mechanisms such as emissions trading can be exploited. Previous regulation of acid rain emissions from the power sector in the US had focused almost entirely on emissions control in new power stations, while existing plants were allowed to operate to whatever standards had applied at the time of their construction. This difference in treatment recognizes the greater costs of retro-fitting emissions control apparatus to existing plant than when emissions controls can be integrated into the design of new facilities, and it also, almost certainly, reflects the greater lobbying power of existing firms compared with potential new entrants. The Acid Rain Program marked a decisive step away from this approach, placing pressure for pollution abatement on plants of all vintages.

The dramatic impact of this shift can be seen in Figure 9. Immediately the scheme began, the ageing, dirty power stations included in Phase I found ways to cut their emissions to an aggregate of 5.3 million tons, some 40% below the cap set by the allowance allocation of 8.7 million tons. This over-compliance continued for the duration of Phase I, demonstrating how, when they had a financial incentive to look, power station operators were quickly able to find unexploited opportunities for large cuts in emissions. By making these cuts early, they were able to build up a substantial bank of unused allowances, that they could then deploy once the even tighter Phase II emissions caps came into operation, either for their own use or to sell. By 2000, the total bank of allowances accumulated during Phase I had reached 12 million tons, equivalent to one year's total emissions. This was then gradually drawn down over subsequent years, so that emissions in Phase II did not completely fall to the level of the new cap until 2006.

Information on the prices at which $SO_2$ allowances were traded provides another perspective on the impact of the programme. Each allowance is worth one ton of sulphur dioxide, either in the year it is issued or in any subsequent year. In principle, the value of an allowance to a power station operator is the cost of cutting its $SO_2$ emissions by one more ton, in other words the marginal abatement cost. If the allowance is used, this cost is avoided; if the allowance is not used, and instead saved or sold, this cost is incurred. Before the Acid Rain Program began, the US EPA had forecast that allowances would probably trade at around $750 per ton of $SO_2$. However, when trading began, the price was much lower – around $150–200 per ton for a number of years.

One reaction to the difference between the EPA's forecast and the market outcome might be that economic forecasting is a mug's game. But here, the basis of price determination should be straightforward: allowances are worth the marginal cost of abatement that would otherwise need to be undertaken if allowances were not used to cover a firm's $SO_2$ emissions. Armed with good technical information on the abatement costs of typical power stations, the EPA should have been in a position to forecast trading prices quite accurately. So why was their estimate so wide of the mark?

Various reasons were suggested by commentators – for example, that state regulation of utilities companies' profits gave them little incentive to try to profit from emissions trading. But work by Denny Ellerman and colleagues at MIT suggests that the main reason was that the forecasts did not anticipate the extent to which emissions trading would stimulate innovative responses which would directly lower abatement costs (and hence permit prices). Under pressure from the $SO_2$ price they now had to pay for each ton of $SO_2$ emitted, power station operators came up with cheap abatement options that had not previously been considered. In particular, railroad freight deregulation in the 1990s had slashed the cost of hauling low-sulphur coal from cheap, distant mines in Wyoming's Powder River Basin, making abatement through input fuel substitution a viable option for many mid-western coal-fired power stations that had previously had no access to cheap low-sulphur coal. The lower-than-forecast permit prices are, on this interpretation, evidence of the strength of the innovation incentive created by market mechanisms.

Having stayed consistently low, at $200 or less since the start of the programme, $SO_2$ allowance prices started to climb at an alarming rate from early 2004 onwards, eventually peaking at almost $1600 per ton at the end of 2005, before plummeting with equal suddenness to a level well below $200 in 2009. What does this startling development, in a previously stable market, reveal about pricing and trading behaviour in emissions trading markets?

One reason for allowance prices to rise in 2004 was that rapidly increasing world prices for oil and gas had encouraged a shift towards coal-fired power generation. This, in turn, increased the prices of $SO_2$ allowances, because of the higher levels of $SO_2$ emissions associated with coal-fired power plants. But the main culprit behind the dramatic 2005–6 price spike in the $SO_2$ market was almost certainly the market's reaction to the discussion of possible changes to the system, which would have cut $SO_2$ emissions still further. Rumours of this possible regulatory tightening sparked vigorous buying and stockpiling of $SO_2$ allowances, in anticipation of their higher future value. Once the new rules were promulgated, this clarified some of the regulatory uncertainty that had promoted precautionary stockpiling of allowances, and allowance prices fell back to lower levels, a trend accentuated in 2008 by the rapidly deteriorating general economic situation, which depressed power demand and hence the need for $SO_2$ allowances.

Two general lessons can be drawn from this episode. One is that emissions trading markets may have an exaggerated reaction to general economic fluctuations. If the supply of allowances is rigidly fixed, changes in the demand for allowances, as a result of general changes in economic activity and electricity demand, can only be accommodated by sharp changes in prices, much greater than in most markets, where higher demand can partly be met by increased supply. For this reason, some have advocated placing 'safety valves' in emissions trading schemes, allowing the authorities to increase the supply of allowances when prices rise beyond a certain point, and reduce the supply when prices fall below a specified floor.

The second lesson is the dangerous impact of uncertainties created by policy-making processes. Discussions about modifications and amendments to the future rules of emission trading systems can have direct and immediate effects on the current market value of allowances, as firms speculate about the implications of future policy change, and perhaps accumulate precautionary stockpiles of allowances. Unlike most other commodity markets, the value of emissions trading allowances is created by policy decisions – and specifically by decisions about the size of the emissions cap – and tinkering with these decisions generates uncertainty about the future value of allowances, with possible costly consequences.

# Chapter 4
# Economic information and values in environmental policy decisions

LORD DARLINGTON. What cynics you fellows are!
CECIL GRAHAM. What is a cynic? (*Sitting on the back of the sofa.*)
LORD DARLINGTON. A man who knows the price of everything and the value of nothing.
CECIL GRAHAM. And a sentimentalist, my dear Darlington, is a man who sees an absurd value in everything, and doesn't know the market price of any single thing.

Oscar Wilde, *Lady Windermere's Fan* (1892)

Chapter 2 described how an economist might determine the desirable level of pollution control, by comparing the costs and benefits of each successive unit of pollution abatement. Some of these costs and benefits are relatively easily measured. Many of the costs of pollution abatement, for example, are the costs of obtaining and installing pollution-control equipment, for which prices are readily available. Others, however, are much less straightforward to include in any cost–benefit analysis. Air pollution, for example, causes health damage. This harm needs to be weighed up against the costs of installing pollution-control equipment, but how do we assess the value of the harm done, in the form of poor health and, possibly, premature death, on a basis that can be compared with the costs of pollution control? In between these extremes, there are many other effects – either costs of control, or benefits of reduced pollution, which cannot be readily read off from available market prices. For example, if high taxes on motor fuel are seen as a way to reduce traffic pollution or congestion, how do we assess the costs to people of forgoing journeys they would otherwise want to make? And if part of the benefit of environmental policy is the preservation of certain natural habitats, how do we value the amenity benefits for walkers and birdwatchers of the unspoiled environment, or the benefits of preserving some biodiversity that could otherwise have been lost?

More fundamentally, in what sense is cost in terms of money values the right yardstick to be using in comparing the advantages and disadvantages of taking action to control pollution? When we consider measures to protect an unspoiled wilderness, or conservation measures that may prevent the extinction of rare birds (or, for that matter, rare beetles), can we really summarize the value of what we conserve, or the destruction that we avoid, in terms of market prices and money values?

## Prices and values in a market economy

Cost–benefit analysis is a technique used by economists to assess whether using productive resources – labour, natural resources, and capital – for some particular purpose is justified by sufficient benefits in return. The idea of cost–benefit analysis has its origins in work in the 1840s by the French economist and engineer Jules Dupuit. Until the 1970s the technique was used almost exclusively to assess large-scale public investment projects – to assess the case for building a bridge or a dam, for example. With the growth of environmental awareness since the 1970s, however, environmental effects have increasingly been incorporated into cost–benefit studies of major projects, and cost–benefit analysis has started to be used much more widely for environmental policy assessments.

The underlying idea of cost–benefit analysis is that using resources always has an 'opportunity cost'. In other words, resources used for one purpose could instead have been used to produce something else. If workers are employed to run a sophisticated system of waste separation and recycling, they could alternatively have been employed in other ways, for example, to build schools or hospitals, or in private sector businesses. What is forgone by using resources for a particular project is, in a fundamental sense, its real economic cost.

To assess the opportunity cost of using resources looks like an impossible task, however. From the thousands of possibilities, how would we know exactly what the alternative uses would have been? Fortunately, in a market economy we have a straightforward starting point. So long as markets for productive resources are competitive, the market prices of labour, capital, and other productive resources will reflect their opportunity cost. Market wage rates, for example, will reflect the opportunity cost of employing labour: businesses will bid to employ labour up to the point where the cost of employing one extra worker equals her 'marginal product' – in other words the extra output she produces. As a result, measuring the cost of resources by their market price summarizes what would otherwise be an impossibly complex assessment of their value in alternative uses.

Cost–benefit analysis tries to draw together a comprehensive assessment of all costs and benefits using the common yardstick of money values, so that ultimately a single calculation can be made of whether costs exceed benefits.

While money values, based on market prices, may be a good reflection of the opportunity cost of resource use, and of the value of goods produced and traded in the market economy, we know that market prices do not always reflect true values. Indeed, environmental economics is specifically concerned with one group of reasons for market prices to be a poor reflection of value, when

he prices of goods fail to reflect the environmental damage caused
by their production. We can also see that many of the benefits of
environmental projects and policies concern things that do not
have market prices at all. We do not buy the air that we breathe, for
example, and there is therefore no market that tells us by how
much the value of clean air exceeds that of polluted air. To
incorporate environmental concerns into cost–benefit analyses we
need to find a way of assessing environmental consequences so that
they can be compared with the assessments of costs and other
benefits expressed in terms of market prices. Put simply, we need
to find a way of valuing the environment in terms of money.

We could of course refuse to do this. We could deny that it is
possible, or that there is any meaning to environmental values
expressed in money terms. We could object that the environment is
beyond price – that our environmental concerns and values cannot
be reduced to something as grubby and sordid as a market price.
This would, however, be unwise. The power of numbers is only too
apparent in public discourse and public decision-making, and
there is a danger that things that do not get measured and valued
simply get ignored. If the environment is to count in public choices,
then it needs to be counted and valued.

It is possible, too, that we are not being entirely honest with
ourselves if we insist that the environment is 'beyond price'.
Beautiful valleys in Wales were flooded when reservoirs were built
to provide clean piped drinking water for the citizens of large
English cities. We may think that this was a mark of civilization
and progress, or we may think that it was outrageous despoliation
of the natural environment. But what is clear is that there was a
choice to be made, between meeting the needs of millions of
citizens and landscape conservation. There were of course other
options. The reservoirs could have been built elsewhere, some with
higher costs of construction and operation, and some which would
have dammed other unspoiled river valleys and landscapes. The
choice that public decision-makers had to make was between

competing claims and needs, balancing landscape conservation, operating costs, and other considerations. Whether they made the right choice or the wrong one is not the point at issue here. What is undeniable is that a choice had to be made between environmental and other concerns, and a balance drawn. The purpose of expressing effects in money terms is simply to be clear about the point at which we are willing to make choices and tradeoffs.

One possibility, of course, if we find it difficult to place a value on the environmental consequences of some policy action would be to measure all of the other, more readily valued, effects, and then ask whether the net effect of these is sufficient to justify the environmental impact. We would still need to compare environmental effects with other costs and benefits summarized in money values, but without necessarily having to put a precise figure on the environmental impact.

Thus, for example, if we consider the consequences of cutting a motorway through the rural landscape depicted by Clare Leighton in Figure 10 (a landscape shaped by human activity but nonetheless of great beauty), we could assess the construction costs of the road and could value the savings in travel time for both private motorists and commercial vehicles. The net effect of these might be a travel time saving well in excess of construction costs, and the question to consider would be whether this gain was sufficient to warrant the environmental destruction that would be required.

Even so, the procedure would be unsatisfactory. For, while individually we might be able to give an answer to this question, the essence of cost–benefit analysis is that it should reflect values held by the population as a whole, not some individual technocratic expert or paternalistic bureaucrat. To do this, we would need to find some way of posing the question to a cross-section of the population.

10. **How much do we value an unspoiled landscape? (The image shows a wood engraving by Clare Leighton (1898–1989) from *The Farmer's Year*, published in 1933.)**

Ideally, too, we would not just want to identify the majority choice, but also to investigate the strength of people's views, so that a majority of people who cared little about the outcome did not necessarily outweigh the more substantial concerns of a minority for whom the outcome mattered a great deal. One of the merits of assessing consequences in terms of values rather than simply on the basis of a majority vote is that values can measure the strength of individuals' preferences, and give appropriately greater weight to those who believe that they would experience substantial harm or substantial benefits, compared to the weight given to those who care little either way.

A controversial feature of money values, however, is that they give greater weight in the final calculation to those whose influence in the market is strongest – to the rich, who have greater purchasing power than the poor. If we ask what people would be willing to pay for some environmental benefit, we are effectively asking what people are willing to give up in order to have it. Other things being equal, richer people would be more able to pay, and would be sacrificing less-valued consumption, than the poor, much of whose income has to be spent on the necessities of life. Willingness to pay for environmental quality will then tend to rise with income, and where views differ about the desirability of possible choices, the preferences of the better-off will tend to be a larger element in the calculation of total value.

In this respect, cost–benefit analysis is like the market economy in general: the rich get to consume more, they get to live in nicer locations, and so on. Views differ as to whether this is a problem for cost–benefit analysis. Some have advocated applying equity weightings in cost–benefit analyses to the effects on people with different levels of income, so as to give a higher weight to the concerns of the poor than the rich, offsetting the initial pro-rich bias in the calculation of total value. The difficulty of course is that views about equity are highly subjective – different people would make very different judgments about the appropriate weightings between rich and poor, and the resulting calculation may be heavily influenced by this controversial adjustment.

An alternative response is to make no equity adjustment, and to treat the cost–benefit analysis like any other decision taken in our unequal, market-based society. Such an approach may be not as indifferent to social inequality as it seems, and this position is held by many economists who care strongly about social justice and equality. They would, however, argue that a cost–benefit analysis, or decision-making about environmental policies, are not the places to address the presence of economic inequalities. Rather, economic inequality should be tackled using the various available redistributive instruments, including taxes and social benefits. Once decisions about the level of redistribution have been made, there is no particular reason to want to deal with equity in relation to the environment differently from equity in any other context. Environmental costs and benefits can then be assessed straightforwardly, on the basis of the sum of individual valuations across all affected individuals.

## Types of environmental value

Before we turn to the available methods for systematic valuation of environmental effects, it is worth reflecting further on different aspects of environmental value. In considering environmental value, economic analysis makes an initial distinction between the value that an individual may place on some aspect of the environment because they themselves make use of it in some way, and values that may be unrelated to individual use.

'Use values', the first category, include the productive value of some aspects of the environment (forests can be managed to provide timber, clean rivers and oceans can provide fish, and so on), and recreational values (people value their visits to national parks, birdwatchers value being able to watch a diverse range of bird species, people can swim from unpolluted beaches). They also include the effects of environmental quality on individual health. In addition, under the heading of use values, we would include the role of the global atmosphere in regulating the climate and of flood plains in reducing the damage from heavy rainfall. In all of these varied ways, individuals 'use' the environment, and they are likely to place value on these uses.

A further category of value, again related to individual use, is the possibility that individuals may value the environment because at some stage they may make use of it, even if not now. This 'option value' may be an important part of the case for maintaining biodiversity, especially in rainforests and other areas rich with plants and animals that might one day provide a source of valuable medicines or other discoveries.

Individuals may also hold 'non-use' values for the environment. People may want to hand on an undamaged environment to their children, or to future generations more generally. There is an element of altruism in this: an idea that people may care for others, and may place value on the environment because they wish others to be able to benefit from it in the future.

Finally, and most controversially, people may hold values for some aspects of the environment that are wholly unrelated to their actual or potential use. I may care about the survival of tigers, pandas, and whales in the wild, not because I anticipate ever deriving use values from them, but simply because they *exist*. It is quite possible that 'existence values' are confined to only a part of the population, and that others only care about the environment to the extent that they actually derive actual or potential use value from it. But it is clear that some people are willing to contribute to conservation projects in areas that they will never visit, and from which they are unlikely to derive any direct use value. If we admit the possibility that people hold existence values for some aspects of the environment, it makes the task of assessing environmental values much more complex. With use values, we only need to survey the likely groups of users (people who go fishing, visitors to national parks, and so on). But existence values may be thinly spread over a widely diverse population with no identifiable links to the environmental asset in question. Also, only some of the available valuation methods have any prospect of identifying the existence value element of total environmental value. Investigating existence values may prove difficult as well as controversial.

## Values inferred from market behaviour

So how then can we find a systematic way of valuing environmental effects, using money as a measuring rod to enable comparisons to be made with other costs and benefits that do have clear market prices? One approach is the statistical technique of 'hedonic pricing', which tries to infer environmental values from observed behaviour in certain non-environmental markets, especially the housing market, and to a certain extent, the labour market. In these markets, we can find situations where environmental goods, while not traded explicitly and separately, are 'bundled together' with traded commodities in observed transactions. Hedonic pricing is a technique for recovering implicit 'prices' for the various attributes of houses or other goods, including implicit prices for environmental attributes.

It is widely believed that house buyers in the UK pay a significant premium for a house located in a school catchment area which gives their children access to a desirable school. Are house prices also affected by environmental aspects of location – for example, exposure to traffic noise, or the presence of an attractive nearby park? Observing that house prices are lower on roads plagued by traffic noise compared with similar houses in quieter streets could, for example, tell us something about how much house purchasers care about traffic noise pollution.

The underlying idea of hedonic pricing is that purchasers of houses (or other complex goods) pay a single price for a package of multiple attributes, each of which influences the overall price. These could include physical attributes of the property (size, condition, the number of rooms, a garden, and so on), running costs (local taxes, likely heating and maintenance costs), locational aspects (being near good public transport facilities, schools and neighbourhood amenities, and being located in a generally desirable area), and aspects relating to environmental quality and amenities (exposure to air and noise pollution, proximity of hazardous or unpleasant industrial activities and waste sites and location in an attractive natural environment).

Prices for houses, as in any market, will be determined by the relationship between supply and demand. Purchasers will be willing to pay more than the average for houses with desirable attributes (such as an extra bedroom, or a garden) and less for

11. How much does traffic noise reduce house prices, compared with similar houses in quieter streets? Houses on the busy North Circular Road at Hendon, north London

houses with undesirable attributes, such as noise from a nearby airport. The result will be that each attribute will bear an implicit price that reflects the willingness to pay of consumers for that attribute. If, for example, the pattern of house prices was such that the implicit price of having a garage was lower than the value of a garage to purchasers, the prices of houses with garages would tend to be bid up in the market until the implicit price of a garage matched purchasers' willingness to pay.

Recognizing that house purchasers might be willing to pay more for an attractive location, or a clean or quiet environment, is one thing. Working out the premium attached to these environmental attributes is another matter, since all we can observe directly is the overall price paid for each property, not separate items for each attribute. Statistical techniques are needed to disentangle the separate components within the overall price of a property – the price of an extra bathroom, etc.

It would be easy to do this if we could find exact comparisons where only one attribute varied at a time. For example, if we could see two houses that were exactly identical in all respects except that one is exposed to traffic noise and the other is not, we could then read off the value of the absence of traffic noise from the premium paid for the quieter property. But houses vary in so many different ways that we can rarely observe such an exact comparison, with only one attribute differing between otherwise identical houses. However, econometric techniques based on multiple regression analysis are available that can identify systematic patterns across large samples of housing transactions, to estimate the impact of each attribute on price, controlling for the other attributes. Or, to put it another way, these techniques can separate out the contribution of each individual attribute to the total price. This results in a set of estimated implicit prices for each attribute, assuming other attributes remain unchanged – in other words, it provides an estimate of the price of one extra bedroom, a larger garden, a quieter street, and so on, *as if these could each be purchased separately.*

Hedonic pricing techniques can therefore give us estimates of the impact of environmental attributes associated with house purchases. This could be a desirable feature, such as the presence of a local nature reserve, or it could be something undesirable such as a nearby landfill waste dump. The question is how much of the total environmental value is captured by this procedure. Specifically, the procedure values only those benefits which residents (or, more strictly, house owners) experience, by virtue of owning the house, and which they would not otherwise experience. A wider group of people may be affected: people may be able to travel from a wide area to visit the nature reserve, and these benefits are not reflected in local house prices; moreover, house purchasers benefit only to the extent that being a resident *increases* the benefits.

Hedonic pricing has been used to estimate the disamenity costs of landfill sites, in terms of the additional traffic noise, odour, litter, vermin, and visual disamenity experienced by local residents. Estimates of landfill disamenity costs could inform cost–benefit analyses of landfill siting decisions. Operating costs (especially the costs of transporting garbage to the site) may be lower if landfills are sited near urban areas, but this needs to be balanced against a greater number of households who would be affected by disamenity costs. Hedonic pricing evidence on the scale of disamenity costs could help to identify the optimal tradeoff between these effects.

Evidence on landfill disamenity costs is also relevant to setting the UK's Landfill Tax at the right level. The landfill tax aims to reflect the environmental costs of landfill waste disposal, relative to alternatives such as recycling and incineration (though ideally it should also be supplemented by a tax to reflect incinerator externalities too). When first introduced, in 1996, the rates applied were £7 per tonne for standard (biodegradable) waste, and a lower rate of £2 per tonne for inert waste, such as building rubble, etc. These rates were set on the basis of research estimates of the external costs from landfill, including the climate change effects of methane and carbon dioxide emissions, transport-related externalities, leaching damage, and disamenity costs. At the time, UK evidence on landfill disamenity costs was not available, and a figure based on US evidence of £2 per tonne was assumed. Subsequent estimates of UK disamenity costs from the Cambridge Econometrics study are not greatly out of line with this. In recent years, however, the tax for standard waste has been raised sharply without reference to external costs, and now (2010/11) stands at £48 per tonne, a level that greatly exceeds the estimated disamenity and other external costs.

One further issue is highlighted by the Cambridge Econometrics landfill study. The study noted that lower-quality housing and poorer communities tended to be clustered near landfill sites. This

## Using hedonic price methods to estimate the disamenity from landfill waste sites in Great Britain

A 2003 study used the hedonic price method to estimate the impact on house prices of proximity to a landfill site, in order to assess the disamenity costs of landfills (noise, odour, litter, vermin, etc).

The study used data on some 600,000 housing transactions over the period 1991-2000, based on the mortgage transactions database of a large UK building society. This provided data on sale prices and house characteristics including the house type, age, floorspace, number of bedrooms, and other facilities. Various characteristics of the local neighbourhood were also reflected in the analysis. Taken together, these factors explained about 80 per cent of the total variation in house prices.

The study then investigated whether any of the remaining unexplained variation in house prices could be accounted for by the presence of a landfill site in the neighbourhood, using data on some 11,000 current and closed landfill sites, and taking account of both the distance of each property from the landfill site, and the size, type of waste, and operational status of each site.

A statistically-significant relationship was found between house prices and the presence of neighbouring landfill sites, after controlling for all other influences on house prices. Being within a quarter of a mile of an operational landfill reduced house prices by about 7%, or an average of £5,500 in 2003 prices, while being between one quarter and half a mile from a landfill had a smaller effect, depressing house prices by 2 per cent. Beyond half a mile landfills had no discernible impact on prices.

The total UK-wide disamenity value of landfills based on these estimates was put at £2.5 billion (in 2003 prices), or about £400,000 per landfill site. This equates to a disamenity externality of £1.86 per tonne of waste.

Source: Cambridge Econometrics (2003)

Economic information and values in environmental policy decisions emphasizes the value of taking proper account of all factors determining house prices. Merely looking at differences in average house prices near landfills, without taking proper account of all other factors affecting house prices, would have been liable to overstate the landfill effect quite significantly.

Quite what generates the tendency for communities living closer to landfill sites to be poorer than the average is unclear. One possibility is that it has to do with processes within the housing market, whereby poorer people are more willing to tolerate the landfill disamenity, for a given price differential, and where house developers tend to recognize that new housing developments near landfills are unlikely to be attractive to wealthy purchasers. But there is some evidence that part of the pattern operates through the political process, whereby richer communities with greater political influence and lobbying skills have been more able to resist proposals for the development of new landfill sites in their neighbourhood.

The housing market is the main source of hedonic pricing evidence relevant to environmental decision-making. The same methodology, however, also underpins some of the most controversial work on economic valuation, that relating to the valuation of changes in mortality risks – sometimes referred to as the 'economic value of human life'. A number of environmental policies, including many relating to local air pollution, can have important implications for human health, and in some cases mortality. Highly polluted air can exacerbate respiratory illnesses, for example, and death rates in the population can rise, especially during periods of particularly high pollution. Measures to reduce air pollution can correspondingly reduce rates of premature mortality, and the question arises of how to take account of this in a cost–benefit analysis.

Estimates of the statistical value of human life (in other words, a reduction of mortality risks equivalent in total to one less death across the population) have been derived from research on a number of areas of human behaviour where individuals choose to expose themselves to activities involving varying degrees of risk. One of these is in the choice of occupation: different occupations vary in terms of the risk of being killed in a work accident or through exposure to various hazards in the course of work. On average (taking account of skill requirements and other relevant factors), there is evidence that more risky occupations have higher wage rates than safer forms of employment. This 'compensating wage differential' has been seen as evidence of the value that workers themselves place on differences in occupational risk – in other words, the additional wage they require to compensate for the additional risk. Estimates in developed countries tend to be high – of the order of $7 million per additional death in the US, for example – and the use of these estimates in cost–benefit analysis tends in turn to place significant weight on pollution control measures that act to reduce mortality risks. The uncertainties around these estimates need to be recognized, but their basis in evidence about what people actually in practice do when confronted with choices that involve differences in mortality risk means that they are more firmly grounded than other available approaches.

## Contingent valuation

An alternative approach to valuing things which are not traded in real-world markets, and which therefore do not have market prices, is to ask people directly how much they would value having more or less of them. For example, a recent Swedish study asked a sample of the population how much they would be willing to pay for a 'predator policy' to secure the long-run survival in the wild of wolves, bears, lynx, and wolverines. There is no actual market where people who value having these species in the wild can express their preferences through payments, and the survey was not actually asking people for contributions. Rather, it was asking the people surveyed to imagine that they were in a situation where they could make a financial contribution which would lead to the survival of these species in the Swedish countryside, and to say how much they would then be willing to pay for this outcome.

This 'contingent valuation' approach is widely used in environmental economics. It can be used to assess values for a much wider range of environmental issues than hedonic pricing techniques, which can only be employed where enjoyment of the environmental good happens to be somehow bound up with a market transaction such as property purchase or rental. It can also be used to assess values for things that do not yet exist, or for changes that are under consideration. Unlike hedonic pricing it can even be used to discover whether people hold 'existence values' for species conservation, threatened landscapes, or historical and cultural sites.

Some examples of where contingent valuation has been used include species conservation, the creation of nature reserves and other amenities, environmental damage from pollution accidents, the provision of different forms of recycling facilities, and improvements in air quality. It has also been used in other fields of economics, for example to assess the potential value of certain forms of medical treatment that might improve individuals' health or quality of life.

Although contingent valuation is versatile and potentially valuable in its ability to reach values that no other technique can address, it has been highly controversial. A major debate in the US was sparked when contingent valuation was used to judge the level of damages that should be assessed for the pollution of the coast of Alaska when the *Exxon Valdez* oil tanker went aground in 1989. The litigation and the report of the commission of enquiry into the legitimacy of this technique provide well-marshalled arguments on both sides of the debate.

Issues about the use of contingent valuation centre on three broad issues – the critical importance of getting the survey design right,

**12. The use of contingent valuation techniques to assess the damage to the natural environment in Prince William Sound, Alaska, caused by the oilspill from the tanker *Exxon Valdez* in 1989, was the subject of intense debate and controversy**

some disturbing puzzles and anomalies that are encountered in results, and the rather disquieting evidence about how people behave in answering surveys based on this method.

It is generally agreed that good practice in a survey of this sort requires the survey interviewer to begin by setting out as clearly and fully as possible the context of the choice that individual respondents will be asked to consider. In the case of many environmental issues, the interviewer may need to explain how the environmental problem is generated, as well as defining carefully the improvement that is being considered. So, for example, a contingent valuation survey to assess the benefits of an improvement in air quality from a significant investment in air

## Contingent valuation of elephant conservation

The willingness to pay of urban residents for conservation of the Asian elephant was investigated in a 2004 study by Ranjith Bandara and Clem Tisdell using the contingent valuation approach.

A sample of 300 residents of the Sri Lankan capital Colombo was surveyed. The participants were presented with background information on the threats to the survival of the elephant population in Sri Lanka, and a detailed description of a possible conservation strategy that could be implemented by a hypothetical agency, financed by a trust fund using voluntary contributions.

They were then asked '*For the next 5 years, would you be willing to pay 500 rupees from the monthly income of your household…towards the establishment of the proposed trust fund…to conserve the elephants in the country?*' Respondents who said '*No*' were then asked the same question, with successively smaller amounts, down to 25 rupees. Those who said '*No*' to all of these amounts were then asked to state the maximum they would be willing to pay.

In all, 93% of respondents were willing to make some payment: 9% were willing to make the highest payment specified; 50% were willing to pay 100 rupees or more; and 89% were willing to pay at least 25 rupees. Average willingness to pay per month was 110 rupees (approximately 1 US dollar), slightly less than 1% of the average respondent's income. Statistical analysis of the factors underlying respondents' willingness to pay found that this was higher among better-off respondents, those with greater literacy and education, and among those with greater awareness of conservation issues.

These results imply that the urban population of Sri Lanka as a whole would have been willing to pay about US$ 90 million in total per year for elephant conservation. This was significantly more than the damage caused by elephants to crops and property in rural areas, in total about US$ 11 million per annum. The authors concluded that a policy of compensating farmers for elephant damage so that they would tolerate the presence of elephants could be viable and justified.

*Source: Bandara and Tisdell (2004)*

pollution control might first need to explain what it is that causes the existing pollution, as essential background to understanding the implications of the choice being offered. Then it would need to define as specifically and precisely as possible the improvement being offered in the survey question. One way this is sometimes done in surveys about improvements in visibility is to show respondents hypothetical 'before' and 'after' photographs with different levels of visibility, and to define the number of additional 'clear' days in the year when visibility would be unimpaired. Providing this information about the context of the survey question and its precise meaning is essential if answers to the survey are to be meaningful, but it is obvious that this must be done very carefully, since there are risks that the interviewer could – unconsciously or deliberately – influence the answers that the respondent gives, by making the description persuasive rather than simply informative.

When we get to the valuation question itself, there are a range of choices, with some significant implications. The simplest question format would be to ask something like: 'Measures are being considered which would improve water quality on this stretch of coastline to a level where it would be safe for public bathing: how much would you be willing to pay for this outcome?' With an 'open-ended' question of this sort, the respondent can make any reply they choose: 'nothing', 'seven pounds', 'two hundred pounds', or any other amount. Analysing the results is then very easy. So long as the sample of individuals questioned is a representative cross-section of the population, the average willingness to pay of the population as a whole is then simply the average of the answers given.

Open-ended questions, where the respondent has to come up with a figure, are these days frowned on by experts in this field, because the evidence seems to be that people struggle with the unfamiliar nature of the question. There are few other contexts in everyday life where we are asked how much we would be willing to pay for something. When we go shopping, we generally see products and their prices displayed, and we choose whether or not to buy something at the price that is advertised. So perhaps it would be more natural to ask contingent value questions in the same way. So, rather than asking 'How much would you be willing to pay?' we should specify an amount. For example, 'Would you be willing to pay ten pounds for this improvement in water quality?' Respondents would then answer yes or no. Unfortunately this is much less informative than the reply to the open-ended question, and analysing the results is much more complex. If respondents answer yes, all that we can conclude is that their willingness to pay is *at least* ten pounds. It could be just ten pounds, or it could be much, much higher. Likewise, if respondents answer no, all we learn is that their willingness to pay is less than ten pounds, and not its exact value. To work out what someone's willingness to pay is, we would have to ask the question many times, with different amounts, until we discover the threshold value where their answer switches from 'yes' to 'no'.

Unfortunately, repeating the question many times to the same individual has been found to risk leading them to an answer that may not reflect their true valuation. Some respondents may get impatient, and switch their answer just to stop the tedious flow of questioning. Others may subconsciously feel that the 'right' answer must lie somewhere among the values offered, with the effect that the sequence of questions influences the final answer.

Whatever the reason, surveys with closed-ended questions that specify a particular amount need to survey many more people to get the same amount of information as with an open-ended question. They may be more reliable, but are also more costly to run.

Experience with contingent valuation surveys has thrown up a number of puzzling anomalies in the way that people respond. Some of these shed doubt on whether responses can really be interpreted as evidence about the value that people place on environmental goods. Some of the anomalous answer patterns are inconsistent with what would be expected if people were making coherent and rational choices, based on a clear underlying set of personal preferences. For example, if people are asked about more than one action in the same survey, the order of the questions seems to influence the results. There seems to be a tendency for people to be willing to pay more for whatever is asked first, and then if they are asked about something else, their willingness to pay declines. Some economists believe that this is evidence that people's answers to contingent value surveys do not really address the actual question being asked, but reflect a 'warm glow' from being willing to do something for the environment, regardless of its content. Their answer to the first question, whatever it is, might include their desire for the warm glow, and their answers to subsequent questions then mean something rather different.

Careful survey design can probe exactly what people's answers mean, and can minimize the extent to which contingent valuation studies are affected by this and other anomalous patterns of individual responses. Nevertheless, the technique remains controversial among economists. Some insist that the various puzzles and inconsistencies found in survey results are evidence that the whole procedure is fundamentally flawed. The answers are unsatisfactory because the process asks people to do something *that they cannot do*, because it is so fundamentally different to anything else that they do in everyday life.

There is no doubt that contingent valuation takes people into unfamiliar territory. They have to answer hypothetical questions about willingness to pay, and this may require them to think about how they make choices, rather than simply to make them. At the same time, they are being asked to make decisions about the value of environmental attributes that they have never had to take before.

The objection that the choices being posed in contingent valuation are hypothetical can be overstated. Certainly, we know that there can be big differences between what people say they want and what they actually choose, and economists generally tend to trust actual actions ('revealed preferences') more than words as a guide to people's real views. Nonetheless, what people say they would do in hypothetical contexts is not wholly devoid of value. A large part of market research for new products is based on asking people whether they would buy a new product before it is actually produced and marketed. Firms are clearly willing to pay large amounts for such studies, and to make costly investments based, in part, on the findings.

One reason that firms place weight on the findings of market research about consumers' reaction to products in hypothetical situations is that the value of the research can be judged against subsequent market outcomes. If market research was systematically misleading about the market for new products, market researchers would be quickly out of business. This observation may give us some confidence about contingent valuation, but it also points to the importance, where possible, of finding other forms of evidence to corroborate the story emerging from contingent valuation research on environmental values. Comparing contingent valuation findings with estimates of environmental value obtained from other methods (such as hedonic pricing, for example) can give us useful information about its reliability, and help us to identify and correct for patterns of error and bias.

# Chapter 5
# The economics of climate change

At the 1992 Earth Summit in Rio de Janeiro, more than 150
countries made a commitment to action to avert dangerous
man-made effects on the global climate, by signing the UN
Framework Convention on Climate Change. They were acting in
response to the growing scientific evidence from the
Intergovernmental Panel on Climate Change (IPCC) that rising
levels of greenhouse gases in the atmosphere, arising from human
activity, were starting to have a noticeable and potentially
damaging impact on the global climate. Further negotiations then
led to the Kyoto Protocol, agreed in 1997, under which a number
of industrial countries took on binding commitments to reduce
their emissions of a basket of the principal greenhouse gases.

The Kyoto target for emissions reductions was relatively small
(a 5.2% cut in emissions by 2012, measured against 1990 levels),
and applied only to the group of industrialized countries that
signed the protocol. Although these countries are on track to
achieve the target, global emissions have been growing rapidly, in
particular because of spiralling energy demand in China and
other fast-growing developing countries.

Against this background of continuing rapid growth in emissions,
attempts to extend and broaden international agreement beyond
the current scope and timescale of the Kyoto Protocol have been

increasingly urgent and fraught. These discussions have been given added impetus by the increasing strength of the IPPC's concern about climate change, based on the accumulating scientific evidence, and, in the UK, by the publication in 2006 of the Stern Review on the Economics of Climate Change, which advocated urgent and significant action.

What, then, are the distinctive issues raised by economic analysis of climate change? How do they inform our understanding of the case for action, and the form that climate change policy should take? Does a consideration of the economic issues shed any light on the prospects for successful agreement on meaningful international cooperation on climate change?

## Greenhouse gases and climate change

Global climate change negotiations are driven by concerns about the process of global warming, which is likely to result from an increased accumulation of greenhouse gases (GHGs) in the atmosphere. The most significant greenhouse gas, in quantitative terms, is carbon dioxide, which contributes about two-thirds of the total global warming impact of greenhouse gas emissions. Human activity leads to carbon dioxide emissions principally through the combustion of fossil fuels – the use of coal, oil, and gas in industrial processes, to generate electricity, as motor fuels, and for domestic heating.

In addition to carbon dioxide, the other significant greenhouse gases include methane, nitrous oxide, and CFCs (chlorofluorocarbons, chemicals used as aerosol propellants, refrigerants, and in various industrial processes). Per tonne emitted, these gases vary widely in the harm they do. Each tonne of methane emissions has an impact on global warming equivalent to 23 tonnes of carbon dioxide, while some CFCs have a global warming potential equivalent to a thousand tonnes or more of carbon dioxide.

Levels of carbon dioxide and other greenhouse gases in the atmosphere have been rising steadily ever since the Industrial Revolution. In 1850, the atmosphere contained some 290 parts per million by volume (ppmv) of greenhouse gases, and this has now risen to 430 ppmv, and is increasing at some 2.3 ppmv annually. Over the course of the 20th century, the Earth warmed by about 0.7 degrees Celsius. The rate of warming appears to be accelerating, with a temperature rise of 0.2°C in each of the last three decades.

Forecasting the growth of emissions and the concentration of greenhouse gases in the atmosphere needs to take account of future economic growth – including the very rapid industrialization of China, India, and other developing countries – and the development of energy technologies. The Stern Review on the Economics of Climate Change summarized the available evidence and estimates. It suggested that future growth in emissions could lead to an atmospheric concentration of 550 ppmv by 2050, and that the annual rate of increase in concentration would by then have reached 4.5 ppmv, and would still be increasing. By the end of the century, atmospheric concentrations could exceed 850 ppmv, more than three times pre-industrial levels.

What this would imply for the climate cannot be the subject of a single projection but requires an assessment of probabilities, because greenhouse gas concentrations at this level are way beyond the range of historical experience. The Stern Review argues that the balance of current scientific evidence indicates that if greenhouse gas concentrations reach three times pre-industrial levels there would be at least a 50:50 chance that the rise in global temperatures above pre-industrial levels would then exceed 5°C.

Although people often talk about 'global warming' and 'climate change' interchangeably, climate scientists and policy-makers are increasingly conscious that the issues are not simply limited to a general rise in global temperatures. Some of the most important issues concern the uneven geographical distribution of climate changes, and the likely increase in climate instability. While global temperatures may rise on average, some areas may become very much warmer, while others may experience less rise in temperature. Effects on the pattern of rainfall may be large and uneven, with possibly drastic effects on the viability of agriculture in some areas. Above all, there is now a recognition that global climate change may involve increased instability in climate patterns, and increased frequency and severity of extreme events – hurricanes, floods, forest fires, and the like.

## What is distinctive about climate change policy?

The structure of the economic issues reflects some key characteristics of the underlying physical processes and the nature of the scientific evidence about them. The problem is generated by an *accumulation of emissions* rather than the level of emissions in any one year, it is surrounded by *substantial uncertainty* about the scale and pattern of effects, there is a possibility of *catastrophic and/or irreversible effects*, and many of the effects of current emissions and policy measures will be experienced in the *distant future*.

The physical process of global warming is a dynamic process, developing over a long time scale, in which damage is done as a result of the stock of carbon dioxide and other greenhouse gases accumulated in the atmosphere, rather than the annual emissions flow. The stock is, of course, the result of past and current emissions. Each year's emissions add a further increment to the stock, in other words to the concentration of greenhouse gases in the global atmosphere. This means, of course, that halting or reversing global climate change will be extremely difficult. Cutting the level of annual greenhouse gas emissions from now on, even quite sharply, may still not prevent increases in the stock of

reenhouse gases in the atmosphere, albeit at a slower rate than
without any emissions cuts.

Atmospheric concentrations of greenhouse gases can be reduced
in two ways. One would be to cut emissions below the level of
natural 'depreciation' of the existing stock, an extremely tall order.
The other would be to take measures to accelerate the removal
of atmospheric carbon. These could include planting forests to
act as 'carbon sinks', that would take a certain amount of carbon
out of the atmosphere, and store it in the timber of the growing
trees. A number of technologies for 'carbon capture and storage'
(CCS) are also under development, although as yet unproven in
large-scale applications. These will probably initially be used to
capture the emissions of large-scale coal-fired power stations,
and store the captured carbon underground, rather than to
withdraw carbon from the existing atmospheric stock. Given that
it will take time to slow the rate of growth of atmospheric
concentrations, and that the scope for 'undoing' the effects of
past emissions is limited, some global warming and climate
change is inevitable.

The fact that the environmental effects of global warming are
generated by the 'stock' of greenhouse gases in the atmosphere,
rather than by annual flows, means that decisions about emissions
abatement involve complex, dynamic considerations. We need to
think about a time profile of abatement, and not just a single
abatement level. A particular target level for the greenhouse gas
concentrations in the atmosphere in 50 years' time could, for
example, be achieved in a number of different ways – by sharp
initial reductions in emissions, by steady reductions in emissions
over the whole time period, or by an accelerating pace of
abatement towards the end of the period. If we assume – probably
quite reasonably – that technological progress will increase the
range of abatement options in future years and reduce abatement
costs, then action now may be more costly than later action. On

the other hand, it would also have earlier benefits, since the level of greenhouse gas concentrations would be reduced earlier.

These issues about the timing of abatement – about the urgency of action – interact with the scientific uncertainties surrounding global climate change. Some of the key uncertainties involve the risks of potentially catastrophic and irreversible changes to the global climate that might be triggered if greenhouse gas concentrations in the atmosphere reach a critical threshold. At some point, global warming could disrupt the deep ocean current that underlie the climatic patterns of many areas of the world – including, for example, the Gulf Stream that gives the UK and western Europe much milder weather than places at a similar latitude on the eastern coast of North America. It is quite possible that this could then generate a chain reaction of adverse consequences which would not be reversed if greenhouse gas concentrations were subsequently brought back down to current levels. However, while it is clear that such a risk exists, it is far from clear when the critical threshold that would trigger such a disastrous chain of events would be encountered. If it is possible that we could be close to the level of greenhouse gas concentrations in the atmosphere that would trigger irreversible changes of this sort, this would be an argument for earlier action, as a precaution against this risk.

Indeed, scientific uncertainty is one of the key distinguishing features of climate change policy. This uncertainty is not the result of bad science, or inadequate research effort. It is inherent in the fact that we are moving into unknown territory, and can only speculate about the effects on the complex and possibly precarious balance of the Earth's ecosystem using what we know from past and current experience. Devoting massive additional resources to a scientific research effort of the highest quality would certainly help us learn more about what is likely to happen, but it would not transform the basic situation. We do not have the option of waiting until the scientific uncertainty is resolved. Instead, we have to make huge, costly, and difficult choices, with far-reaching implications for humanity, in the face of unavoidable uncertainty about the scale, speed, and in some cases even the direction of effects. What is more, we are unlikely to find out where the truth lies until it is too late to do much about it.

Few public policy decisions involve this degree of uncertainty, and there is no other context which combines such uncertainty with such large costs stretching into the indefinite future. Whatever we do – taking action or doing nothing – will be a large gamble. One of the most telling contributions of the 2006 Stern Review on the Economics of Climate Change was to point out that this unique decision requires decision-making methods that take proper account of the extensive and irreducible uncertainty about the processes of global warming and the consequences of policy action. In particular, we should avoid analyses, and decision-making procedures, that collapse the wide range of possible developments too quickly into a single 'best guess' forecast, on which our attention then focuses. This is tempting: summarizing the evidence into a single point – a single forecast number – makes the discussion much easier to focus, and avoids the risk that people pick and choose between the range of scenarios to find the one that suits their interest or their existing preconceptions. However, concentrating attention on the 'best guess' trajectory is dangerous if it leads us to neglect the risk of low-probability developments involving large costs.

## Future generations

In one other crucial respect, global warming is unlike any other major public policy decision. A huge part of the damage from global warming – and hence the benefits from any policy action taken now – would be borne by future generations, including many generations as yet unborn. When judging how much action we should take to control current emissions, how can we properly reflect the interests of future generations? On what basis should we weigh the interests of future generations against the interests of the current generation, who will have to bear substantial abatement costs, while not living long enough to experience many of the benefits?

Economists tend to think of policy measures which involve costs and benefits which arise at different times in terms of *discounting*. The usual context, of course, is one in which both costs and benefits are largely experienced by the current population. A project to build a dam or bridge would require an initial investment, and yield benefits in future years once the project was complete. The current generation forgoes some consumption now, in order to provide the resources for the project, but also reaps subsequent benefits. A cost–benefit analysis of the project would assess both the costs and the benefits in terms of their present values, in other words, their equivalent value in the current year. Discounting future benefits means valuing each pound's worth of benefits experienced in some future year at a lower value than the equivalent benefits experienced in the current period; a discount rate of 3% would effectively reduce the value of future benefits by 3% for each year the benefits lie ahead.

The justification for this approach is that it reflects the way in which individuals in the population make similar choices. (As we discussed in Chapter 4, the whole philosophy of cost–benefit analysis is that it is trying to summarize the values held by the population as a whole, and not to impose some arbitrary 'expert' or 'elite' views and preferences.) We see individuals making choices that imply some preference for consumption now rather than an equivalent amount of consumption in the future. We can also think of possible reasons that might explain this. People may simply be impatient – they may genuinely prefer consumption now even if that means reduced consumption later – or they may realize that if they defer consumption to the future there's always a risk that they may not be around to enjoy it. The risk that you might die in the meantime would be sufficient reason for a rational person to discount future benefits by on average some 1% per year or so, reflecting the average annual risk of death. A further reason for people to discount future benefits is that they may anticipate being better-off in the future, so that any given amount of consumption will tend to add less to their standard of living than it would if consumed now, while they are poorer. Incomes have risen steadily over the last century, and it would be reasonable to believe that this long-term trend will continue in the coming century; in these circumstances, some discounting of future benefits would be justified. Taken together, these various reasons for discounting might justify applying a discount rate of some 2% to 4% per annum to future benefits, in assessing public projects over 'normal' timescales.

But only parts of this logic apply to projects – such as the control of climate change – where a large part of the benefits would be enjoyed by generations as yet unborn. All of the current generation of voters and policy-makers will be gone by the time many of the benefits are experienced. Impatience cannot be a reason for discounting benefits in this case, nor does the risk of mortality apply in the same way. There therefore seems to be less reason to discount future benefits over this very long timescale. However, if we decide to apply a discount rate that is very much lower than the rate that would be applied to shorter-term projects, the implications are enormous.

At a high rate of discount, costs and benefits in the distant future become vanishingly small in a cost–benefit calculation, but with low discount rates (or no discounting at all) costs in the distant future exert a large influence on cost–benefit assessments. For example, a discount rate of 4% per annum would mean that £1,000-worth of benefits in 100 years' time was worth only £20 now, while a discount rate of 1% would imply that it was worth £370 now, 19 times as much in present value terms as with the 4% discount rate. Without any discounting at all, of course, it would be worth exactly the same now, £1,000, as in 100 years' time. Applied to calculations of the costs and benefits of policies to control global climate change, significant discounting would mean that benefits in the very distant future can be largely disregarded. By contrast, with a low discount rate (or no discounting at all) the interests of distant generations would dominate the overall calculation.

Ultimately, the issue is one of intergenerational equity: how much should we be prepared to leave for future generations to enjoy? The Stern Review takes a very strong ethical position on this question, arguing that there is no reason to favour the interests of the current generation over any other. Stern consequently applies a low discount rate to future benefits, with the effect of giving the interests of generations in the distant future a heavy weighting in the calculation of overall costs and benefits. Other economists, including the US economist William Nordhaus, one of the Stern Review's sharpest critics, have argued for significantly higher rates.

## The economic case for climate change policy

Climate change policy involves costs and benefits – the abatement costs that will be incurred in reducing greenhouse gas emissions, and benefits in the form of reduced climate change damage. We can use the economic framework set out in Chapter 2 to assess the reduction in emissions of carbon dioxide and other greenhouse gases that would be justified in terms of the environmental benefits achieved. In this framework, abatement is worthwhile up to the point where the marginal cost of abatement equals the marginal environmental damage – in other words, where the cost of reducing greenhouse gas emissions by one further tonne is just equal to the reduction in climate change damage achieved by that additional tonne of abatement. One factor determining how much abatement is justified will then be the pattern of abatement costs – in particular, how steeply marginal abatement costs rise as we seek greater abatement.

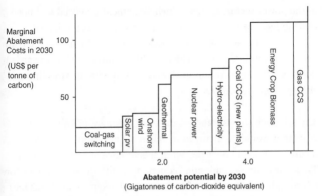

13. Global marginal abatement cost curve for carbon emissions from power generation, 2030

Figure 13 illustrates marginal abatement costs in the electric power industry, one of the main contributors to carbon dioxide emissions. The schedule takes a 'bottom-up' approach, using estimates of the abatement potential and abatement cost for each of the principal options for reducing carbon emissions from electric power generation. These include renewables such as wind, biomass, and solar power, nuclear power, and the use of carbon capture and storage to reduce carbon emissions from fossil fuel power generation.

Given the long lead time in the construction of power plants, especially new nuclear capacity, and the long time horizon over which climate change policies will need to operate, the schedule looks forward to costs and abatement potential in 2030, rather than now. This inevitably is speculative. Renewable energy technologies are developing rapidly, and the costs of abatement using these technologies will almost certainly fall quite significantly between now and 2030, as a result of scale economies and cost-saving technological changes, though it is impossible to pin a precise figure on the abatement cost reduction. In addition, many factors will affect the 'baseline' level of activity and emissions in the power sector, against which abatement potential will need to be judged. More rapid economic growth, for example, will increase the baseline level of emissions, but would also be likely to increase fossil fuel prices, which could encourage a shift towards non-fossil-fuel generation in any case, even without any climate change policy measures.

The schedule shows some estimates of the marginal abatement costs that would be incurred in achieving emissions reductions below what would be expected in the absence of policy measures. Thus, for example, emission reductions by the global power sector of around 2 Megatonnes of carbon-dioxide-equivalent ($MtCO_2e$) per year could be achieved at a marginal abatement cost of less than \$40 per tonne of carbon. Doubling this level of abatement would increase marginal abatement cost to some \$85, requiring use to be made of more expensive abatement options. It is interesting to note how the various different technologies compare in terms of abatement costs. On the estimates used in Figure 13, nuclear power comes out as a significantly cheaper way of cutting power sector emissions than carbon capture and storage per tonne of reduced carbon emissions. However, speculating about the costs of technology twenty years ahead is inevitably imprecise, and the estimated marginal costs are sufficiently close that relatively small additional improvements in costs for one or two generation technologies could radically change the overall cost ranking of measures.

Accepting more nuclear power as the price of controlling climate change is, of course, one of the most controversial issues in current energy policy. While focusing on climate change we should not neglect the potential external costs of nuclear power, in the form of the risk of a catastrophic nuclear accident, along the lines of the Chernobyl accident, or the disaster narrowly averted at Three Mile Island. The risk of such a disaster may be very low, but it would be foolish to claim that it is zero, and the costs of a large-scale disaster would be high and long-lasting. The difficulty, of course, is in placing any numerical value on the probability of such an accident, and hence in assessing the size of the nuclear risk externality.

Outside the power sector there are significant opportunities for greenhouse gas abatement in other industrial sectors, especially in iron and steel, cement, and chemicals manufacture. The transport sector has substantial – and rapidly growing – emissions, and a range of possibilities for reducing emissions from road transport and aviation. Carbon abatement in agriculture and forestry could include the possibility of planting new forests as carbon 'sinks'. Reduced energy use by private households could also contribute considerable emissions reduction.

In principle, we could add all of these areas of possible abatement to the power sector diagram in Figure 13, to construct an overall economy-wide marginal abatement cost schedule. In practice, however, this is rarely done. Most analyses of global abatement potential and costs perform much the same calculation, but embedded in the inner workings of a large-scale simulation model, rather than summarized in a single graphic.

Some studies have suggested that a significant amount of carbon abatement could be achieved at zero or negative marginal cost – in other words, there are measures which would both cut carbon emissions and at the same time save money compared with the technologies that would otherwise be used. This has been controversial. If they really are cheaper, why would they not be used already by profit-seeking firms? It has been argued that there are various forms of barrier and market failure that sometimes prevent efficient decision-making by firms. Poor information, for example, might mean that some cheap low-carbon options are ignored, and that firms simply choose the technologies with which they are familiar. Action to improve the availability of good technology advice and information would then have a double benefit – firms would make higher profits, and carbon emissions would be reduced. Others, however, think this is rather too good to be true, and that there could be important hidden costs which are being missed when the costs of technologies are being compared.

Assessing the damage costs of climate change also has features which arouse controversy. The scientific uncertainties relating to the physical processes, and the fact that these go beyond the range of recent experience, makes it difficult to be at all precise about the relationship between greenhouse gas emissions and some of the key factors affecting climate change damage costs. In particular, we know little about the precise point at which major threshold effects such as the reversal of deep ocean currents would be encountered.

One of the most thoroughly researched categories of climate damage cost is the impact on agriculture. Agricultural production will be affected by changes in temperature, sunshine, and rainfall; in some colder regions, these changes may boost agricultural output, while agriculture would be severely harmed by higher temperatures and more severe water shortages in places which are already hot and dry. Climate change is likely to involve unpredictability in weather patterns and an increased frequency of hurricanes, droughts, and other severe weather events, and these will tend to harm agriculture, through more frequent crop failures and loss of harvests. There are, however, some offsetting benefits to crop growth from higher levels of carbon dioxide in the atmosphere. What is crucial in assessing the overall pattern of effects on agriculture is to take account of the adjustments and adaptations that can be made, as farmers switch to cultivating the most suitable crops for the changed climate in their region. If we simply assume that farmers in each region go on planting the same crops as they do now, we will exaggerate the adverse impact of climate change on agricultural output.

Climate change is likely to affect the availability of water supplies more generally. Water supplies in already-arid areas will become even more scarce. In southern Europe, for example, an increase in global temperatures of 2°C could lead to a reduction of between 20% and 30% in summer rainfall, exacerbating existing water-supply problems.

Energy requirements for heating will fall, but the energy needed for cooling and air conditioning will rise, especially in parts of the world where temperatures are already close to the limit of human tolerance.

More frequent and severe floods, storms, and hurricanes will damage homes and infrastructure. Costly investments may need to be taken to reduce these costs and risks – for example, in improved storm drainage and other defensive measures. As the polar ice melts, the rising sea level will increase the risk of coastal flooding, creating a need for major investments in flood defences. For example, more than £125 billion of buildings and other assets in London lie in the area that would be exposed to greater flooding, and the existing London flood defences, including the costly Thames Barrier, will eventually prove insufficient and will need to be strengthened.

Almost all of these costs are likely to bear disproportionately on poorer countries. They are more dependent on agricultural production, and many are in warmer and tropical locations where the effects will be more severe. In most developing countries, too, the economic system is less flexible, and will struggle to adapt to the changing circumstances. Some of the poorest countries will be particularly badly hit. A large part of Bangladesh, home to some 160 million people, already lies close to sea level, and without massive flood defences will be inundated when the sea level rises. As climate change becomes more severe, the costs of population displacement and conflict caused by rapid changes in climate and living conditions in different parts of the world could pose a major threat to social and political stability well beyond the countries most directly affected.

14. A woman carries children away from her home after massive flooding in Bangladesh. Climate change is expected to increase the frequency and severity of floods, and sea level rise will inundate a large part of Bangladesh

One useful way of summarizing the total effect of all of these costs is by calculating the 'social cost of carbon' – in other words, the total damage caused by one more tonne of carbon emitted into the atmosphere at a particular point in time, expressed as a monetary value. The social cost of carbon can be calculated for emissions now, or at some future date. Typically the social cost of future emissions will be higher than of emissions now because damage is caused by the accumulation of emissions in the atmosphere. Estimates of the social cost of carbon for current emissions have a wide range. A survey by the UK economist David Pearce in 2005 found that most estimates of the social cost were rather low – between $4 and $9 per tonne of carbon, expressed in terms of year 2000 prices. However, many of these omitted the costs and risks of catastrophic outcomes, and are therefore likely to be underestimates. A study by UK government economists had proposed that a much higher figure of £70 per tonne (about $105 per tonne) should be used for the social cost of carbon in UK policy assessments. The Stern Review on the Economics of Climate change assessed the social cost of carbon under 'business as usual' at the even higher value of $312 per tonne. By contrast, William Nordhaus, a critic of the Stern Review, estimates the current social cost of carbon at about $30 per tonne.

Faced with such extraordinary disagreement, what should we conclude? Do we simply fall back on our prior beliefs and personal inclinations, picking the result that best suits our preconceptions? Do we dismiss all of the estimates on the grounds that environmental economics clearly has nothing useful to tell us, if it cannot agree on a calculation of critical importance for the most significant environmental policy decision of our time? Or does the diversity itself carry an important message, which we should investigate?

If we look more closely at the reasons that underlie these diverse results for the social cost of carbon, we can see that they reflect important differences in approach and judgment. One thing they reflect is the inherent uncertainty in global warming policy: we do not know enough about the science to eliminate imprecision about the risks and scale of various effects. They also reflect different approaches to analysing this uncertainty. In particular, Stern places greater weight on exploring the consequences of a wide range of scenarios, rather than focusing on a single central case, or a few variants. Taking proper account of some of the downside risks is something that Stern does thoroughly, and is one reason that Stern's estimates are higher than earlier work.

But, above all, the estimates vary because they take different positions on some crucial ethical choices that have to be made in formulating policies towards global climate change. These include how effects on rich and poor are weighed up in the calculation, and how the interests of future generations are represented. The UK government economists' study applies a significant 'equity weighting' which accounts for about half of the total estimated social cost. The aim of this is to assign a greater

15. **The Thames Barrier, built in 1984 to protect London from the risk of flooding, at a cost of over £530 million. Rising sea levels due to global warming will require many such investments**

weight to effects which fall on poorer countries than if we simply look at effects in terms of current money incomes and exchange rates.

The Stern Review, as already mentioned, takes a particularly distinctive position on the issue of discounting future costs and benefits, arguing that the interests of future generations should be weighted almost as heavily in the calculation as the interests of current generations. Many commentators on the Stern Review have pointed out that the rate at which Stern discounts future costs and benefits is a major reason why the Stern Review's estimate of the social cost of carbon is so much higher than others. Sensitivity calculations published by the Stern team themselves show that their estimates of the costs of climate change are more than halved if the discount rate is raised by a single percentage point.

What do these assessments imply in terms of policy action? Here it may be interesting to compare the contrasting policy prescriptions of the Stern Review and its critic William Nordhaus. Despite their disagreement about discounting, both agree that climate change is a serious issue, requiring large adjustments in the global economy.

Despite its lengthy and controversial analysis of the costs of climate change and the impact on future generations, the final policy prescription from the Stern Review comes from a rather more direct observation. Stern argues that the accumulating scientific evidence indicates that allowing greenhouse gas concentrations to exceed 550 ppmv would be dangerous, and would expose humanity to an excessive risk of seriously damaging outcomes. Stabilizing at this level would require emissions to be cut by about 25% by 2050, measured against the current level. This is more drastic than it sounds, since growth in the world economy over the next 40 years would lead to substantial growth in emissions in the absence of any policy intervention. To achieve this emissions reduction, the rate of emissions per unit of output would in fact have to be cut by 75%, a drastic reduction in the carbon footprint of economic activity. The Stern Review argues that abatement costs for this target would however be small – about 1% of total global output annually. The Review suggests that might be considered a rather low insurance premium against a risk of a catastrophic climate outcome, which in unlikely but not inconceivable worst-case scenarios could wipe off 20% or more from global output and living standards. The Stern Review argues that early action to cut emissions would sharply reduce the costs of making this major adjustment in emissions. Delaying action would increase the risk of irreversible damage to the climate, and would mean that the world economy would continue to invest in power stations and other long-term energy projects on the basis of current high-carbon technologies.

William Nordhaus, by contrast, argues for a climate change 'policy ramp', which would initially seek rather modest emissions reductions, which would then build up over time. His estimates of the optimal policy would seek emissions reductions of 15% now, 25% against business-as-usual by 2050, and 45% against business-as-usual by 2100. Because of the growth in emissions that would occur without any policy intervention, these reductions in emissions against a business-as-usual baseline (that is, against a baseline without any policy intervention) would actually imply some continuing emissions growth, measured against current levels, albeit at a lower rate than would otherwise occur. One reason for Nordhaus's slower rate of emissions reduction is the higher discount rate which he uses, of 4% compared with the 1.4% used by the Stern Review. This reduces the urgency of action, because it makes postponing abatement costs more attractive, while at the same time giving lower weight to the future costs of the increasing concentration of greenhouse gases. Nevertheless, while Nordhaus advocates a slower policy build-up than the Stern Review, he agrees with Stern that climate change is a cause for real concern. Sooner or later significant policy intervention will be required to achieve large cuts in carbon emissions.

## Pricing carbon

How do we achieve the substantial reductions in energy consumption and carbon emissions that will be needed if we are to reduce the risk of severe climate change? What can we do, individually and collectively?

One way of looking at the problem is in terms of technologies and technological solutions. For example, we can discuss the saving in energy consumption that could be achieved through sophisticated household energy-management systems, new motor vehicle technologies, or greater use of public transport. We can consider how much of our electricity needs could be met from renewable sources such as wind and solar power. Low-carbon technologies exist, more will be developed in future, and their costs are likely to fall with mass production.

Another way of looking at the problem, which preoccupies economists, is to think about how we can get these things to happen. It is all very well having the technology. We need to ensure that there is a reason for people to *use* it.

Some part of the shift towards low-carbon technologies and reduced carbon consumption can be achieved through individual action by citizens and socially concerned businesses. Survey evidence shows that many people say they are willing to make changes in their consumption if it will benefit the environment, and some people are willing to make more drastic lifestyle choices to reduce or eliminate their individual carbon 'footprint'. At the same time, however, private motoring, air travel, and the level of material consumption have risen steadily, even in those countries where public concerns about global warming are strongest. Part of the problem may be a difference between what people say in surveys and what they do in practice. As we saw in Chapter 4, surveys need to be designed very carefully if they are to uncover people's true willingness to pay for environmental action.

The scale of the required reduction in carbon emissions is massive, and may be well beyond what people imagine when they say they are willing to make changes for the sake of the global climate. There also may be a natural – and entirely rational – individual reluctance to take action when other people do not. An individual's actions make a truly negligible contribution to the reduction of climate change, whereas the actions of thousands of millions of people would make a real difference. Also, the carbon footprint of individuals is extraordinarily complex. Correctly calculated, it would include not only their direct purchases of fuel and power, and their journeys by car and plane, but also the energy that has gone into producing the goods and services that they consume, all the way back through the many stages in the production chain from raw materials production to the finished product. Efficient and effective action to reduce carbon emissions needs to be spread across all areas of energy consumption, both by industry and individuals, but also to focus on the particular areas where the greatest difference can be achieved, at the lowest possible cost. The concerned citizen might quite reasonably feel bewildered by the complexity and scale of the problem.

To rely on voluntary action by individuals will be insufficient to achieve the major changes needed. Governments will need to intervene to ensure that enough action is taken by both individuals and industry to achieve the necessary emission reductions. The analysis of instrument choice in Chapter 3 is then directly relevant to climate change policy decisions. What instruments are available for governments to use in climate change policy, and what are their relative merits?

To date, the climate change policies of most countries have relied heavily on conventional 'command-and-control' instruments which directly regulate emissions or technology choices. Through the existing regulatory regimes, many countries have instructed industry to adopt certain specific low-carbon equipment and processes. Similarly, governments have required households to make use of products that will reduce energy use or carbon emissions – for example by ending the sale of conventional incandescent lightbulbs, to ensure that households switch to low-energy alternatives. These forms of direct regulation have the disadvantage that they tend to be inflexible, one-size-fits-all solutions which do not take account of differing circumstances. As Chapter 3 showed, this inflexibility carries with it the risk of excessive costs, higher than the minimum needed to achieve the desired environmental outcome.

Market-based instruments have also been used to discourage fossil fuel use. Carbon taxes have been introduced by a number of European countries including Sweden, Norway, Finland, the Netherlands, and Denmark. Some countries have raised existing energy taxes or introduced new ones. The European Union introduced a Europe-wide emissions trading system for carbon dioxide in 2005, and some other countries have followed suit with similar arrangements. These market-based policy innovations have been controversial, and in some countries have been met with extremely hostile lobbying from industrial interests.

Nevertheless, despite the real political difficulties and some economic obstacles, it seems clear that pricing measures of some sort (either in the form of carbon taxes or emissions trading) must inevitably form part of the long-term policy package, if significant reductions are to be achieved in the use of carbon-based energy. Reducing emissions of carbon dioxide sufficiently to halt the rise in atmospheric carbon dioxide concentrations will require far-reaching changes in patterns of energy use, and, more fundamentally, in patterns of human activity. Conventional regulation could only achieve changes in fossil fuel use on the scale required through intrusive intervention into the detailed workings of the economy, on a scale that risks clogging up the efficient functioning of the economic system. The essence of a market economy is that individual choices are guided most efficiently through the price mechanism. By incorporating systematic carbon-saving incentives into prices, through taxation or emissions trading, the millions of decentralized economic decisions made every day can reflect the true social cost of carbon emissions.

## A carbon tax

A carbon tax works by taxing fossil fuels in proportion to carbon content. Per unit of energy, coal is taxed more heavily than oil and natural gas, while non-fossil-fuel sources of energy are untaxed. Burning fuel containing a given quantity of carbon leads predictably and unavoidably to a given amount of carbon dioxide emissions, so that a tax on the carbon content of fuels is almost equivalent to taxing carbon dioxide emissions themselves. With the exception of carbon-capture-and-storage technologies that may shortly become available for power stations no viable end-of-pipe cleaning technologies for carbon dioxide emissions are currently available.

Taxing carbon would encourage energy users to substitute away from high-carbon energy sources towards fuels with lower emissions per unit of energy. If levied on the fuels used by power stations, for example, a carbon tax would encourage a shift away from power generation using coal towards oil and gas, and even more strongly towards untaxed renewables (wind and wave power), and towards nuclear energy.

In addition to encouraging substitution away from high-carbon fossil fuels, a carbon tax would reduce energy consumption overall, since it would raise overall energy prices. Fossil fuel prices would rise because of the tax, while many of the non-fossil-fuel alternatives are, as we have already seen, more costly sources of power. As a result, overall energy consumption would be reduced, an effect which would arise through three main channels.

First, households and business would reduce their direct use of energy. If taxes make energy more expensive, householders might, for example, turn their central heating thermostat down and live in a slightly colder house, in order to save on fuel costs. Likewise, if the tax on motor fuels was increased, people might drive less, perhaps switching to public transport.

Second, higher energy prices would stimulate improvements in energy efficiency, for example through household insulation, and through the replacement of old central heating boilers and other energy-using equipment with new equipment performing the same function with less energy.

Third, higher energy prices on production of goods and services would feed through to higher prices for goods and services which require a lot of energy, directly or indirectly, in their manufacture. The price of a mobile phone, for example, includes an element reflecting the price of each of the materials and components used in production. One of these is copper. Its production uses a lot of energy, and a carbon tax on the energy used in copper production would raise the cost of copper to the phone manufacturers, and in turn raise the cost of mobile phones. The same will be true of the costs of all the other materials and components that go into manufacturing a mobile phone. In total, the effect of the carbon tax will be to raise the price of a mobile phone by an amount reflecting the total carbon used in its production, both directly by the phone manufacturer and indirectly in the production of materials and components. If a carbon tax increases the price of mobile phones sufficiently that consumers buy fewer of them, this would lead to reductions in carbon emissions at all stages in the production chain.

One of the attractions of charging for carbon through a carbon tax or other carbon pricing is that it naturally stimulates this wide range of behavioural responses throughout the whole economic system, rather than focusing on the more limited set of actions that can be directly regulated by government. Using carbon pricing to incentivize changes in behaviour is a clear example of how the flexibility offered by economic instruments can reduce the overall cost of achieving a given environmental outcome. Faced with the higher price, individuals cut their consumption – of fossil fuels and of goods produced using fossil fuels – if there are cheaper alternatives. If there are no satisfactory alternatives, or if the alternatives would be more costly, then they are not forced to take action. Pricing carbon in effect offers a safety-valve that avoids excessive costs in achieving the overall reduction in carbon emissions.

## Carbon emissions trading

As we have seen in Chapter 3, emissions trading has very similar properties to emissions taxation. Carbon emissions trading offers an alternative way of using the price mechanism to discourage carbon emissions. By placing a cap on permitted carbon emissions – or equivalently on the use of fossil fuels – carbon emissions trading ensures that tradeable carbon emissions permits have a positive price. The price of carbon permits then functions in an almost identical way to a carbon tax, discouraging the use of fossil fuels, and raising the prices of goods and services produced using carbon-intensive production processes. The most significant application of emissions trading to date has been the EU Emissions Trading System, but its effectiveness has so far been somewhat mixed.

The EU Emissions Trading System covers the power sector and $CO_2$-intensive industries (iron and steel, cement, pulp and paper, and similar), a total of around 10,000 plants across the EU, which together account for almost half of the EU's total emissions of carbon dioxide. It began operation in 2005, for a first three-year trading period (2005–7), and Phase II (2008–12), which includes the deadline for meeting the Kyoto targets, is now under way.

Allowances were distributed free to existing firms in Phase I, but a small proportion have been auctioned in Phase II. For the third phase, beginning in 2013, the European Commission has proposed that a substantial proportion of allowances should be auctioned to generate revenues for member state governments.

The process within the EU ETS for determining the overall emissions cap and allocating allowances was curiously decentralized. The EU-wide cap on emissions emerged as a result of 'National Allocation Plans', formulated by member states, which determined the quantity of allowances to be allocated to their firms. The result of this decentralization was the absence of any clear debate about the EU-wide cap that should be placed on emissions. In the first phase, in particular, some countries made unduly generous allocations, without meeting any rigorous challenge from the EU. In the second phase, the EU was more active in challenging proposed allowance allocations, and the proposals for the third phase, to begin in 2013, envisage that the EU will take over responsibility for allowance allocations and enforce a tighter cap on emissions.

For Phase I, the allowance cap is widely regarded as having been too permissive, and $CO_2$ emissions in practice were well below the cap. Some allowances remained unused at the end of the period, and once this was realized by market participants, the allowance price dropped to zero. There is some debate over the impact of Phase I on emissions, and about whether the surplus allowances were entirely due to over-generous allocations, or at least in part might have reflected greater-than-expected abatement. The evidence seems to point to a mixture of these effects, although the emissions reductions achieved by the first phase were probably rather modest – perhaps a 2% cut in emissions compared with what would have occurred in the absence of the ETS.

In Phase II, the overall cap looked tighter, and there was initially an expectation that it would achieve significantly greater emissions reductions. However, this hope has been undone by the recession, which has led to a significant fall in energy demand and consequently emissions, for reasons unconnected with the ETS. Again, the decline in ETS allowance prices is evidence that the system is not significantly constraining emissions – prices have fallen from €30 per tonne at the start of Phase II to around €15 per tonne in late 2010.

At the same time, even though the EU ETS has so far failed to achieve major cuts in emissions, it has had dramatic effects on energy prices. Allocating allowances for free meant the system did not add to the total costs of industry as a whole. On the other hand, it did make using carbon expensive for individual firms. Unused allowances could always be sold, and using allowances then has an opportunity cost, in the reduced profits from selling unused allowances. Electricity producers, in particular, recognized that the costs of additional production had effectively risen, and increased electricity prices to reflect this. Power companies' profits rose sharply following the introduction of the EU ETS, because prices had risen to reflect the market value of allowances used in generation, while at the same time the system had supplied generators with free allowances sufficient to cover most of their needs.

Despite the difficulties that the EU ETS has so far experienced in establishing significant and durable price incentives to reduce carbon dioxide emissions, the underlying structure of the system (apart from the decentralized cap-setting) is very similar to that of the successful system of sulphur dioxide trading under the US Acid Rain Program, discussed in Chapter 3. In principle, if a tighter cap can be set on emissions, the EU ETS offers the possibility of establishing a significant and broadly spread incentive for carbon emission reductions across a very wide range of economic activity, and on a common basis throughout the EU.

## Obstacles to price instruments

One major barrier to using carbon pricing or taxation to reduce industrial emissions of greenhouse gases has been vocal opposition from industry groups, concerned that the additional costs to industry would harm the competitiveness of firms in international markets. If European countries levy a carbon tax on industrial energy use while other countries do not, European firms will have to compete with firms from outside Europe that do not bear the same carbon tax burden. Much the same concerns have been raised about auctioning carbon permits: industry will have to pay more for its energy, and this may harm its ability to compete.

The rhetoric from industry lobbyists on this issue has been insistent and influential, but economists are in general very sceptical about this line of argument, for two main reasons. One is that it tells a partial story. Any revenues from carbon taxes will permit other taxes to be reduced, and the net effect on industry as a whole could therefore be easily offset by reductions in other taxes paid by industry – such as the payroll taxes on employment. The second reason is that it neglects the possibility of exchange rate adjustments, which would act to offset the higher costs of production. Taking both of these offsetting factors into account, a carbon tax would still be likely to reduce the competitiveness of carbon-intensive industries and firms, but by less, while low-carbon sectors of industry would actually gain more from the adjustments than they would lose in carbon tax.

A second political obstacle to high carbon taxes is the impact on the living standards of poorer households. In the cold, damp climate of northern Europe, energy for heating may be almost a necessity, and spending on energy can take up a large part of the total budget of poorer households. Increasing the tax on energy will then hit poorer households proportionately harder than those on average incomes and the better-off, for whom energy is a much smaller component of total spending. However, as with taxes on industrial energy use, it is a one-sided analysis to focus only on the extra energy taxes paid. Taxes on household use of energy or carbon would raise substantial revenues, and these can be used to finance reductions in other taxes that could substantially offset the adverse impact on the living standards of poorer households.

## Non-price instruments

Despite these arguments, concerns about the effects of carbon taxes on industrial competitiveness or on poorer households may still place political constraints on how much use can be made of carbon taxes and pricing to reduce greenhouse gas emissions. It may then be attractive to look for instruments that would supplement energy pricing, particularly those which will increase the carbon savings achieved by any given level of taxation.

As already observed, the pace of development of low-carbon and zero-carbon technologies will determine how far and how fast the world can hope to reduce carbon emissions. Placing a significant price on the use of carbon will, in itself, encourage more rapid carbon-saving innovation. In addition, measures to accelerate the development of low-carbon technologies will widen the scope for industry and households to reduce their energy consumption, by offering low-carbon alternatives to existing industrial and household equipment. Government subsidies can speed up programmes of scientific and industrial research and development, and if publicly supported innovations are made generally available, this will encourage more rapid diffusion of the new technologies than if they had been privately financed and patented for private profit.

In some areas of energy use, there are concerns that even existing energy-saving technologies are not being used to their full potential. There are often concerns, for example, that both households and industries have been slow to make use of technologies that improve energy efficiency. This may be because of poor information, or because not all the benefits can be captured by the person making the investment (a landlord who insulates a flat may not be able to let it at a higher rent to recoup the insulation costs, even though tenants could find that their energy bills were reduced), or because some households or businesses simply cannot afford to finance the up-front costs of energy-efficiency investments. Some of these barriers can be traced to various forms of 'market failure', and there are good reasons for governments to try to correct this market failure through various forms of policy intervention. These have often included things like information campaigns, free energy-efficiency advisers, tougher building regulations to enforce higher standards in new houses, 'home energy ratings' so that prospective tenants or purchasers of houses can see the energy running costs of the property, and loans or grants to people otherwise unable to afford energy-efficiency investments.

However, a word of caution is needed about energy-efficiency policies. They seem to hold out the promise of relatively cheap and guaranteed emissions reductions, without some of the adverse social impacts that might arise from high-energy taxes. Supplying households with low-energy lightbulbs, for example, seems to offer guaranteed and quantifiable reductions in energy consumption: a 20-watt low-energy bulb offers much the same light output as an old 100-watt incandescent bulb, and thus seems to offer the potential to reduce energy consumed by domestic lighting by 80%. But this purely technical estimate of energy savings neglects possible consumer responses, and these may offset some or all of the energy savings. In effect, what more energy-efficient equipment does is reduce the price of heating, lighting, and the other services supplied by energy-using appliances. If the cost of lighting is cut by 80%, households may choose to have brighter lights, or to leave lights on for longer, and these responses would reduce the savings. Likewise, some part of the gains from better home insulation might be taken in increased comfort, by turning the thermostat up, rather than entirely in lower bills. Only if energy-efficiency improvements are accompanied by higher energy prices can we expect that this so-called 'rebound' effect on consumption will be neutralized, and that improving energy efficiency will reduce energy consumption and carbon emissions.

## International climate negotiations: prospects for success

Global warming is a global problem. Emissions contribute equally to damage regardless of their source: a tonne of carbon dioxide emitted from the US or Europe is no more or less damaging than a tonne emitted from China or India. Likewise, the damage experienced by any country is a function of global emissions. Individual countries' emissions or abatement affect the level of climate change damage they experience only through their impact on the concentration of greenhouse gases in the global atmosphere. The global nature of the problem calls for corresponding global action if the risk of catastrophic climate change is to be tackled effectively.

The need for coordinated international action is even more pressing than in the case of European acid rain policies discussed in Chapter 2. In the acid rain case, there was at least some reason for a country to take unilateral action, based on its own domestic costs and benefits. If international negotiations failed, the default position would thus be some level of national abatement, albeit on a smaller scale than the ideal level. In the case of global climate change, countries gain negligible benefit from their own abatement, because the effect on the global climate is determined by the total stock of greenhouse gases in the atmosphere. Cuts by any individual country acting alone can only make a trivial dent in this total stock, and although the total worldwide benefit from a country's actions may be enough to warrant the abatement costs it would incur, the proportion of the total worldwide benefit that the country itself would experience would be so small that – to all intents and purposes – the country would have incurred abatement costs but received no benefits in return.

International agreement is thus indispensable to effective action on the scale required. Although some countries, under popular pressure, committed to national actions on climate change even before any international agreement, no country acting alone can make any meaningful impact on the process of climate change. The Kyoto Protocol, agreed in 1997, made a first step towards coordinated international action, but the only binding emissions reduction targets it set were for industrialized countries, and the largest emitter, the United States, stayed outside the agreement. The lifespan of the Kyoto Protocol comes to an end in 2012, and international negotiations in recent years have aimed for a successor agreement that would have a much broader membership, a longer time horizon, and a commitment to substantial emission reductions.

Ideally, the international agreement needs to encompass all countries, since this would spread the burden of carbon abatement costs most widely, and hence reduce the costs that each country needs to bear. However, getting countries to sign up to an agreement is made difficult by the temptation of free-riding. For any country, staying outside an international agreement on climate change offers the prospect of benefits without costs. A non-signatory avoids incurring any abatement costs, but would still experience all of the benefits from greenhouse gas abatement measures undertaken by those countries that do sign up to the agreement. All countries experience the same process of global climate change, and the benefits of policy action cannot be restricted in any way to those countries that have shouldered the burden of carbon abatement. This is an immense obstacle to achieving a broadly based international programme of coordinated policy action.

Even where pressure from concerned citizens and voters at home and diplomatic pressure from countries abroad encourages countries to sign up to an international agreement on climate change policy, the temptation of free-riding remains a problem. Countries may sign but take little effective action, calculating that any penalties for breaking the terms of the agreement would be less than the saving in abatement costs, and probably largely unenforceable as well. Realizing this, other countries may be tempted to free-ride too. After all, the worst outcome for any country is to incur the costs of abatement, but find that so few other countries have done so that there are no benefits to be gained in return. With these temptations, the coalition of countries taking action might prove unstable, and unable to persuade power generators and others to make the long-term financial commitments required for renewable energy, carbon capture and storage, and other expensive carbon-reducing investments.

Reaching a comprehensive global agreement is also complicated by the great differences between countries. Some countries are much more vulnerable than others to climate change, especially low-lying countries which are at risk of sea level rise, and countries whose current climate provides high agricultural yields, which could be at risk if the climate becomes more unstable. On the other hand, there are some countries which might even stand to benefit from modest climate change.

Carbon abatement costs vary across countries too, and any agreement should ideally ensure that carbon reductions take place where they can be made most cheaply. In the Kyoto Protocol, this was reflected in various 'flexibility mechanisms', which were intended to allow countries to pay for carbon reductions elsewhere, where this would be less costly than their own abatement. These have been controversial, partly because it is difficult to ensure that these mechanisms always achieve genuine emission reductions that would not otherwise happen.

But the most crucial difference between countries is in current emissions per head of population, with rich countries responsible for much higher carbon emissions, relative to their population size, than poorer countries. On average, energy-related carbon dioxide emissions were 4 tonnes per head of population across all countries in 2002, but three times this level (11.7 tonnes) in the industrialized member countries of the OECD, and barely half this level (2.2 tonnes per head) in developing countries. Emissions in the USA, the world's largest economy, exceeded 20 tonnes per head. Given this variation in emissions levels, a central focus of controversy underlying the international negotiations on climate change has been how the burden of achieving a global cut in emissions should be shared between countries. What target for emissions cuts should be given to countries with different levels of emissions per head – and different levels of income and living standards?

One option – though clearly unrealistic – would be to ask for equal percentage cuts in emissions against the baseline of current emissions levels. Then, if emissions were to be cut by half, for example, the abatement required of the USA per head of population would be almost ten times the abatement required in developing countries. But it would also leave the USA with emissions ten times higher than developing countries, and would condemn developing countries to permanent energy-constrained under-development. Also, developing countries might observe that they were being asked to contribute to solving a problem that they had not created through their past emissions.

An alternative would be to agree that all countries would be awarded the same per capita carbon budget (say 4 tonnes per head), which would permit some growth – and emissions growth – in developing countries, while concentrating nearly all abatement in the richest industrialized countries. Perhaps this solution might seem fairer – though judgments about fairness in this situation do seem particularly subjective. However, by concentrating abatement actions in a relatively small group of countries it runs the risk that they will perceive the agreement to involve costs which exceed their own benefits. Ultimately, countries only sign up to international agreements when it is in their interests to do so, and an agreement which loads too much of the cost on one group of countries is almost certain to fail.

The obstacles to reaching a successful climate change agreement are real and substantial: both the temptation of free-riding and disagreement about burden-sharing pose major challenges. Despite the large measure of scientific agreement about the growing risks of climate change – as reflected in the increasingly urgent tone of the reports from the Intergovernmental Panel on Climate Change – the 2009 summit in Copenhagen which was intended to agree a successor to the Kyoto Protocol failed to reach any meaningful deal on coordinated action. Environmental economics cannot sidestep the negotiating realities – any more than the extensive scientific evidence has done. But it can provide evidence that the scientific case for action is matched by a convincing economic case that the long-run benefits of action will be greater than the costs of carbon abatement. Equally importantly, it has helped to show how policy instruments such as emissions trading and taxation can provide the market signals that will be needed to steer the global economy towards a low-carbon future.

# References and further reading

## General recommendations

Oxford Review of Economic Policy, issues 14(4) *Environmental Policy* (1998); 19(3) *Controlling Global Warming* (2003); 24(2) *Climate Change* (2008).

There are many good academic textbooks on environmental economics. As a follow-up to this introduction, I suggest Tom Tietenberg and Lynne Lewis, *Environmental and Natural Resource Economics*, 8th edn. (Pearson Addison-Wesley, 2009). This also provides a good introduction to the economics of depletable and renewable natural resources.

## Chapter 2: The economic theory of efficient pollution control

Dieter Helm (ed.), *Economic Policy Towards the Environment* (Blackwell, 1991).
The seminal paper on Coasean bargaining is R. Coase , 'The Problem of Social Cost', *Journal of Law and Economics*, 3 (1960): 1–44.
The discussion of acid rain policies in Europe draws heavily on David M. Newbery, 'Acid Rain', *Economic Policy*, 11 (October 1990).
On the economics of international environmental policy agreements: Scott Barrett, *Environment and Statecraft* (Oxford University Press, 2003).

## Chapter 3: Environmental policy: instrument choice

European Environment Agency, 'Using the Market for Cost-Effective Environmental Policy, Market-Based Instruments in Europe', EEA Report No. 1/2006 (Copenhagen: EEA, 2006).

Paul R. Portney and Robert N. Stavins (eds.), *Public Policies for Environmental Protection*, 2nd edn. (Washington, DC: Resources for the Future, RFF Press, 2000).

Winston Harrington, Richard D. Morgenstern, and Thomas Sterner (eds.), *Choosing Environmental Policy: Comparing Instruments and Outcomes in the United States and Europe* (Washington, DC: Resources for the Future, RFF Press, 2004).

A. Denny Ellerman, Frank Convery, and Christian de Perthuis, *Pricing Carbon: The European Union Emissions Trading Scheme* (Cambridge University Press, 2010).

The account of the US Acid Rain Program draws heavily on A. Denny Ellerman, Richard Schmalensee, Elizabeth M. Bailey, Paul L. Joskow, and Juan-Pablo Montero, *Markets for Clean Air: The US Acid Rain Program* (Cambridge University Press, 2000).

## Chapter 4: Economic information and values in environmental policy decisions

David Pearce, Anil Markandya, and Edward Barbier, *Blueprint for a Green Economy* (London: Earthscan, 1989), Chapter 3: 'Valuing the Environment'; Chapter 6: 'Discounting the Future'.

David Pearce, 'Cost–Benefit Analysis and Environmental Policy', in Dieter Helm (ed.), *Environmental Policy: Objectives, Instruments and Implementation* (Oxford University Press, 2000).

Symposium on Contingent Valuation, *Journal of Economic Perspectives*, 8(4) (1994): 3–64.

Richard C. Porter, *The Economics of Waste* (Washington, DC: Resources for the Future, RFF Press, 2002).

The hedonic pricing study of landfill disamenity discussed is Cambridge Econometrics, *A Study to Estimate the Disamenity Costs of Landfill in Great Britain: Final Report* (Defra Publications, 2003).

The contingent valuation study of elephant conservation discussed is R. Bandara and C. Tisdell, "The net benefit of saving the Asian elephant: a policy and contingent valuation study", *Ecological Economics*, 48 (2004): 93–107.

## Chapter 5: The economics of climate change

Dieter Helm (ed.), *Climate-Change Policy* (Oxford University Press, 2005).

Nicholas Stern, *The Economics of Climate Change: The Stern Review* (Cambridge University Press, 2007).

Mark Maslin, *Global Warming: A Very Short Introduction*, 2nd edn. (Oxford University Press, 2009).

William Nordhaus, *A Question of Balance: Weighing the Options on Global Warming Policies* (Yale University Press, 2008).

# Index

Environmental Economics